Missing in Connecticut

Missing and Unidentified People

1886 -2011

GEN@4

Michael C. Bouchard

Dedication

Irene LaRosa
March 01, 1971 (Missing)

Susan LaRosa
June 23, 1975 (Missing–Homicide)

This book is dedicated to Irene LaRosa and Susan LaRosa, who inspired this book. Their life was too short and their age too young, but for those they touched, you understood the quality of their existence, which will far exceed the evil that took them.

"And do not fear those who kill the body but cannot kill the soul. Rather fear him who can destroy both soul and body in hell." (Matthew; 10:28).

i

Copyright

Disclaimer

The author had no previous knowledge of any of the cases in this book, The information contained in this book was obtained from local newspapers articles, online sources, court documents, vital records, annual census, personal biographies, archival reports, and interviews with family members, and other persons with knowledge.

A reasonable attempt was made to verify all the information in the book. However, some data could not be verified because of the elapsed time.

There were conflicting stories told during the interview process, and other persons with knowledge did not want to cooperate in the research.

The information extracted from older reference documents has been reworded to clarify the older terminology used.

The author exercises the right not to print sensitive, personal, or information having evidentiary value.

While being interviewed, individuals' statements were made voluntarily with the knowledge the accounts may be printed in this book in their original context.

The statements made during the interviews were the beliefs and opinions of the person being interviewed; the accounts do not necessarily reflect the author's personal views.

During the interviews, individuals reported conflicting facts compared to other statements made by others; the author takes no responsibility for the contradictory information provided during the interviews.

Newspaper articles included in this book include personal information that had already been distributed to the public based on known facts at the time of print. The author holds no responsibility for names or other personal data in newspaper articles or online sources.

The author takes no responsibility for incorrect information provided during personal interviews or from outside resources.

Table of Content

Table of Content

Table of Content

Table of Content

Table of Contents

Introduction

I have investigated almost one hundred missing juvenile cases; fortunately, most cases were solved without incident over a short period.

My interest in missing a person's cold cases began during the research for my first book, "The Disappearance of Denise Lloyd Martin" (Bouchard, 2016).

This book aims to overview the more than one hundred-five active missing persons and unidentified cold cases in Connecticut from 1886 to 2011.

Missing person cases are prioritized by the "Solvability Factor." Although time works against us in solving these cases, it should not discourage us from finding the truth or pursuing those who perpetrate such crimes.

Unfortunately, Connecticut's State Police cold case task force has been disbanded over the years due to the lack of funding, which requires smaller understaffed police departments to investigate existing cold cases without the staffing or funding.

I noticed several missing people reports and serial killings in Connecticut during the 1960s, and 1970s, many of which have gone unsolved over the decades.

The book includes interviews with members of the LaRosa family of Vernon, Connecticut. Irene LaRosa had gone missing in 1971, and Susan LaRosa had disappeared in 1975; her body was later found in a wooded area of Vernon, Connecticut, in 1978

Introduction

The interviews with family members identified two possible family members and an ex-brother-in-law as possible suspects in the disappearances of both Irene and the homicide of Susan LaRosa.

The interviews also suggest a possible link between the LaRosa disappearances and the disappearances and homicides of other young white females missing in the Vernon area between 1968 and 1978.

The book discusses the annual number of missing people throughout the United States. The reason for the disappearances, prolonged grief, and post-traumatic stress suffered among relatives of missing persons, identifying criminal profiles and algorithms patterns of suspects, and the inherent need to continually update missing person cold cases.

In many older cold cases, the primary suspect had died, and there was no judicial resolve or answers for family members.

I want to express the urgent need for people withholding information about criminal cases to contact the authorities. If you wish to stay anonymous, send a message to my email (forevernightct1@comcast.net), and I will forward the information

It is a heavy burden for a person with knowledge of a horrific crime not to talk about it, but by withholding the information, a person is as guilty as if they had committed the crime themselves.

Missing by the Numbers

For whatever reason, a missing person whose status, alive or dead, cannot be determined.

People go missing for several reasons. The person may walk away and adopt a new identity, the person may become lost or involved in an accident where the body is not found, or the person may have become a victim of a crime, and the body may be hidden.

It is estimated that approximately 800,000 children go missing in the United States annually, including children who have run away voluntarily. The number of children missing in the United States is a concern; the numbers suggest a child goes missing every forty seconds.

Even more concerning is that 76.2% of children abducted by strangers are murdered within three hours after being kidnapped.

On average, it takes authorities two hours to gather accurate information from panicking parents or relatives before the investigation.

Approximately 2,300 people are reported missing each day.

The Native American populations in the United States seldom report lost or missing people. Missing person cases often receive low priority by the law enforcement community, especially when they are over eighteen years old or are known to be involved in criminal activities.

The Office of State Medical Examiners holds 40,000 unidentified skeletal remains throughout the United States.

It is estimated over eight million children go missing worldwide each year. There are 100,000 active missing person cases in the United States annually.

The human trafficking industry's growth has drastically increased the number of missing children cases worldwide. Most missing adult cases are made up of people suffering from either substance abuse problems or mental health issues or are victims of a crime or bad homelives.

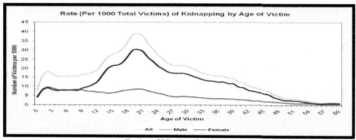

(Ratio of Victims by Age)

Reasons Why People Disappear

There is no one reason people disappear; there can be more than one contributing factor in many cases.

The author has sub-categorized and defined a list of possible reasons why a person might disappear; regardless of why a person goes missing, it is law enforcement's responsibility and the public responsibility to be vigilant in their attempts to locate these individuals.

Sub-Categories of Disappearances:

Criminal

Abduction:	A juvenile is abducted by a non-custodial person.
Abduction:	A juvenile is abducted by a parent or relative.
Kidnapping:	An person is abducted by an unknown person.
Homicide:	A person attempts to hide or destroy the body.
Seizure:	Government officials abduct a person.
Sold:	A person is sold into slavery for serfdom, sexual exploitation, or free labor.

Personal

Runaway:	A juvenile without notice, leaves their home or institution.
Escape:	A person leaves to escape abuse by a parent, guardian, or responsible for their care, spouse.
Escape:	A person attempts to flee criminal apprehension.
Religious:	A person joins a cult or organization which requires no contact with the outside world.

Personal

Identity: A person leaves and assumes a new identity and
                 life.
Suicide: The individual chooses a remote location to spare
                 the family from trauma.

Medical

Mental: A person not of cognizant mind wanders away
                 without knowledge of identity.
Medical: A person wonders or dies due to a medical
                 condition due to the lack of medication.

Weather-Related

Weather: A person goes missing as a result of inclement
                 weather conditions or disaster.

Long-Term Effects on Family Members and Friends of Missing People

I think homicides and missing person cases are the two most devastating crimes that family members and law enforcement communities must endure.

The family members of a homicide victim grieve the loss of their loved one, but on the other hand, the family members of a missing person suffer but then must live with the unknown fate of their loved one.

When searching for a missing person is over, and the media has gone, the victim's family members and friends must begin a new life, wondering about their loved one's fate. One day their life was ordinary, and each day will never be the same.

A person's disappearance can have a profound emotional effect on family members and friends. It is estimated that twelve people are affected by the disappearance of a person. The impact on these people can be emotional, psychological, physical, and in some situations, financial.

In some cases, family members and friends begin to suffer from depression, anxiety, hysteria, and other psychological disorders resulting from the disappearance.

Most people perceive an abduction as a single-victim crime, but it is a multi-victim crime affecting several people for prolonged periods. In many cases, the parents, siblings, relatives, and friends die, not knowing their loved one's fate.

Individuals impacted by a person's disappearance live in a void referred to as "Living in Limbo" (Holmes, 2008). The term "Limbo" refers to avoiding a person's physiology or emotional state, which exists between grief and loss (Wayland, 2007).

Unfortunately, during this phase of grief and loss, there are patterns of hope, if only brief, in which the person believes that some sort of closure is possible.

In many cases, family members, siblings, relatives, or friends live with false feelings of guilt, believing they could have done something to prevent the disappearance.

In the LaRosa cases, Irene LaRosa's (1971) disappearance and the disappearance and murder of Susan LaRosa (1975) have divided the family. Some refuse to admit family members were involved in the crimes, while others want justice.

In the Dennis Lloyd Martin case (Disappeared from Great Smoky Mountain National Park; 1969), the Martin family will not discuss Dennis's disappearance even among family members (Bouchard, 2016). Many of Dennis's family members have died, not knowing Dennis's fate.

I can say nothing that will take away the grief and pain people experience when a family member disappears. Still, I can promise to do whatever I can as a police officer and author to help update leads in existing cold cases to locate the missing person and prosecute the offender.

"A mystery is only a mystery until it is solved."

Calculating Suspect Patterns and Algorithms

Attempting to detect specific crime patterns and criminal profiles can be daunting; however, once a model is identified, the information can be used to anticipate, prevent, and sometimes solve cases.

Data input about specific crime types within a geographical region can detect crime patterns, identify suspect psychological profiles, and identify the suspect's Modus of Operandi.

Child abductions are divided into two classifications. The first and most common child abductions are committed by family members. In most cases, it violates a custodial decree, which involves some concealment, flight, or an attempt to deprive someone of their custodial rights. There is no anticipation of injury to the child (Hammer, Finkelhor, and Sedlak, 2002).

The second and most dangerous type of child abduction is committed by strangers or an acquaintance of the victim. It occurs when a child is taken by physical force or the threat of bodily harm by an unidentified person (Hammer, Finkelhor, and Sedlak, 2002).

The psychological profile which motivates the stranger offender to abduct a child is significantly different than that of the family abductor.

The family abductor often believes they are removing the child from an unsafe environment. The stranger abduction is motivated by sexual desires and control, with the offender having no conscious concern about inflicting injury or death on the victim.

The typical stranger abductor is usually a white male in his 20s or 30s; the offender will most often victimize the child; the victim's age range can vary from young children to teenagers. When any child abduction occurs, authorities must work fast and diligently to gather information immediately and begin the search.

Children are often abducted within a quarter mile of their home or school, with most cases being sexually motivated. It is estimated that strangers or acquaintances commit 25% of annual child abductions in the United States.

On average, 99.8% of missing children are found; a large percentage of these disappearances result from juvenile runaways.

As a school resource officer, we were taking two or more missing juvenile reports a week was not uncommon.

In these cases, the child would voluntarily walk out of the school or home to meet with friends; however, even in these cases, the investigation must be started immediately and handled diligently if the disappearance has a criminal aspect.

In an adult disappearance, many victims are involved in illegal drug or alcohol use, prostitution, suffering from mental health issues, or have a history of criminal behavior. These individuals are often victims of criminal acts.

Estelle Landers-Lang and Sherron Lang (Child)

Missing: July 06, 1944

Hartford, Connecticut

DOB: Estelle 1917

DOB: Sherron: 1938 (Child)

Landers-Lang is a 29-year-old petite white female with brown hair and brown eyes.

Landers-Lang's daughter (Sherron Lang) could only be described as a 6-year-old white female.

Landers-Lang and her daughter (Lang) may have been victims of the Ringling Brothers and Barnum Bailey Circus tent fire, which occurred in Hartford, Connecticut, on July 06, 1944.

The fire killed168 people.

Some of the bodies were identified by the state Medical Examiner; however, many of the bodies were so severely burnt; it was impossible to identify them correctly.

Estelle's mother, Gertrude Landers (Wyandotte, MI), reported her daughter Estelle might have been missing as early as 1942. Gertrude said Estelle had left her daughter's father four years before the fire.

Estelle married her husband, Richard Lang, in 1936 but divorced him in 1940. Gertrude Landers explained her daughter Estelle "Loved to wander" and did not stay in one place for long.

It was later discovered that the 200' x 425' carnival tent had been cleaned and treated with a flammable paraffine liquid containing gasoline before the fire.

In 1950 Robert Dale Segee of Circleville, Ohio, a 21-year-old lighting crew worker at the carnival, had set the fire.

Segee's told the authorities "That an apparition of an Indian on a flaming horse would often visit him."

(1944 Barnum Tent Fire)

Segee later recanted his confession because he said the police told him he was guilty, so he confessed to the crime. Robert Segee was suspected of other arson fires and homicides; he was eventually sentenced to two 22-year prison terms.

Estelle Landers-Lang and her daughter Sherron Lang are still considered missing, and the case remains open.

The state has reopened the case and is now conducting DNA testing on several of the unidentified remains.

Constance Christine Smith (aka Connie)

Missing: July 16, 1952

Salisbury, Connecticut

DOB: July 16, 1942

Connie is a 10-year-old white female, 5-0" tall, 85 pounds, with light brown hair, blue eyes, glasses, and a scar under her right nostril.

Connie was last seen wearing a long-sleeve red zipper-down windbreaker, a brown banana halter top, navy blue shorts with plaid cuffs, tan leather shoes, and a red hair ribbon; Christine's clothes all had name tags sewn inside.

Connie lived in Sundance, Wyoming, at the time of her disappearance but was spending part of her summer at Camp Sloan in the rural village of Lakeville, located in Salisbury, Connecticut.

At the time of Connie's disappearance, Smith's parents were divorced, her father lived in Wyoming, and her mother was visiting her parents in Greenwich, Connecticut. Connie was the granddaughter of former Wyoming Governor Nels H. Smith.

It was reported on the evening before her disappearance Connie had fallen in her tent, bruising her hip while involved in horseplay with tent mates; Connie was given an ice pack at the camps dispensary to help with her bruised hip.

On the morning of her disappearance, Connie was involved in a physical altercation with her campmates and sustained a bloody nose. Connie was nearsighted, and her glasses may have been broken during the fight.

At approximately 8:00 am, Connie told her tent mates she was skipping breakfast and returning the ice pack to the camp dispensary. Connie left the ice pack in her tent and began walking toward Indian Mountain Road.

Connie was observed leaving the camp by caretaker August Epp misidentified Smith as an older camp counselor and did not report seeing her leave the camp until police questioned him.

Connie was seen by Alice Walsh on Indian Mountain Road. Connie had stopped at Walsh's house, asking for directions. Walsh said Connie appeared to be crying. It is believed Connie was being bullied at the camp, and she may have been attempting to walk to Lakeville Center to use a telephone to call her parents. The camp officials discouraged the use of the phone.

Hobb Hortman and his wife observed Connie walking on Route 44.

It's believed Smith continued to walk north on Route 44 before stopping at the Deep Lake farmhouse to ask for directions. After asking for directions, Smith continued to walk toward the Lakeville Center.

(Newspaper Article – Connie Smith)

A pair of farmhands mowing hay near Belgo Road, who had been working late that night, had been questioned by authorities if they had seen Connie; neither had.

Frank Barnett was the last to see Connie at 08:45 AM; he said it seemed like Smith was looking for a ride. It was reported that Smith was seen getting into a car on Route 44 near Belgo Road.

At the time of her disappearance, Smith may have been carrying a black zipper purse containing photographs of her friends; she did not have any money or clothes.

On July 16, 1952, camp counsels discovered Connie missing when her tent mates returned to their tent and found Connie's ice pack still on her bed.

An extensive area search was conducted, but no trace of Smith was found. People of interest were interviewed about Connie's disappearance, but no one has been charged.

15

Other individuals claimed responsibility for Connie's abductions, but their confession was later found to be lies or hoaxes.

In 1953 Fredrick Walker Pope confessed to the authorities that he and a man named Jack Walker had abducted Connie, killed her, and then buried her in Arizona.

It was later discovered Pope had fabricated the stories as a hoax.

In 1957 convicted sex offender and killer George Davies confessed to murdering Connie Smith. Davies was on death row for killing 16-year-old Gaetane Boivin in Waterbury, Connecticut. On May 09, 1957, Searchers found her body twelve days after her disappearance.

Davies's second victim Brenda Doucette of Bristol, Connecticut, was found on May 14, 1957; Doucette had been abducted while walking to school. Doucette had been strangled with a man's sweater and stabbed twenty-two times.

At the time of the murders, Davies was a paroled sex offender. Davies later recanted his confession about murdering Connie, saying he made up the story to prolong his execution date. Davies was executed on September 20, 1959.

In 1962 the Connecticut State Police were alerted to a young girl's (Little Miss X) body found in Coconino County, Arizona.

In 1953 Fredrick Walker Pope confessed to murdering Connie and burying her in Arizona; Connie and (Little Miss X's) dental records were compared; however, an identification was never made.

Years later, an attempt was made to exhume and extract DNA samples from (Little Miss X) to compare with Connie Smith. However, Coconino County authorities could not locate (Little Miss X's) burial site.

Frances L. Tuccitto (aka Frances L. Hubbell)

Missing: June 01, 1953

Portland, Connecticut

DOB: 1910

Tuccitto is a 34-year-old (deceased) white female 5-02" tall, 100 pounds, with brown hair and brown eyes. Tuccitto is missing one of her fingers due to a factory accident while working at Russell Manufacturing Company (Middletown, Connecticut).

Francis married Joseph V. Tuccitto in 1929. The Tuccitto's had resided in several locations in Middletown, Connecticut, before moving to 17 Commerce Street (circ. 1940) in Portland, Connecticut. Tuccitto's husband, Joseph, never remarried; he died in March of 1956 at the age of 49, three years after his wife disappeared.

The Tuccitto's left behind five children: Angelica, Joseph (deceased), Sebastian (deceased), Lucille (deceased), and William Tuccitto. There is no additional information concerning Frances Tuccitto's disappearance.

Anna Bertha Kenneway (aka Anna Bertha LaValle)

Missing: June 04, 1954

Manchester, Connecticut

DOB: 1912

Kenneway is a 42-year-old (deceased) white female, 5-04" tall, 155 pounds, with brown hair, blue eyes, and pierced ears.

Kenneway was last seen by employees at Pratt and Whitney's aircraft in East Hartford, Connecticut. Kenneway's husband of twelve years, Philip Kenneway, was a machine operator at Pratt and Whitney.

Philip never contacted the police about his wife's disappearance, but he did tell his wife's son Richard LaValle (Son from his first marriage), about the disappearance.

Philip told her son that he and Anna were involved in an argument that day, so he left the house and went to the movies between 7-9 pm. Anna's son Richard posted a classified ad in The Hartford Courant in July 1954, asking his mother to contact him in Webster, Massachusetts.

LaValle had been in the Worchester Hospital recovering from injuries sustained in a motor vehicle accident at the time of his mother's disappearance. Anna Kenneway lived on Little Street in Manchester, Connecticut, at the time of the disappearance.

Philip Kenneway said when he returned home from the movies, he noticed his wife had taken clothes, three thousand dollars in cash, nine thousand dollars in bonds, and a religious statue. The statue was probably the weapon used in her murder.

Kenneway's neighbors reported Anna and her husband, Philip, were constantly arguing and, in some instances, were involved in physical altercations.

Kenneway's neighbor Frank Duncan, age 92, moved next door several months before Anna Kenneway went missing. Duncan said it was an odd relationship. "They both worked the third shift at Pratt and Whitney, and he (Philip) would charge her a buck a week to ride with him to work."

Duncan recalled that Anna brought half a cake she baked to his house to give to his wife; Anna explained: "I'm not going to give him (Philip) the other half; that's mine."

Duncan said Philip never mentioned Anna's disappearance. He "Never mentioned anything about it."

Before Anna's alleged disappearance, she called a coworker (Ruth Skinner) and told her she was thinking about leaving her husband.

Family members and coworkers reported that Kenneway was not the type of person who would get up and leave.

Philip Kenneway obtained a divorce from Anna Kenneway in January of 1956, two years after Anna's alleged disappearance.

Duncan recalled after the divorce, Philip came running over with the court papers and exclaimed, "Now I'm free."

In 1991 Anna Kenneway was legally declared dead after her survivors petitioned the Manchester Probate Court.

The Kenneway case was reopened in 2006 at the request of Kenneway's granddaughter Anita Wilson.

19

The cement garage basement of Kenneway's Little Street residence was poured by Philip Kenneway when his wife disappeared.

Philip Kenneway was suspected of burying his wife's body under the garage. The police dug up the garage, but Anna Kenneway's body was never found.

Kenneway's family members always suspected her husband, Philip Kenneway, of her murder; Philip Kenneway died in 1995 at 80.

John Xavier Gaydosh (aka John Thomas Gaydosh Jr.)

Missing: June 01, 1963

New Britain, Connecticut

DOB: 1934

Gaydosh is a 30-year-old white male 6-0" tall, 190 pounds, with brown hair.

Gaydosh's disappearance is suspicious because he was involved in a $75,000-dollar lawsuit against Salvatore DiPillio, the owner of a building located at the time of his disappearance at1197-1209 Main Street, Hartford, Connecticut.

According to court records (New Britain Superior Court), On July 06. 1956 a lawsuit was filed against DiPillio by the Gaydosh. Gaydosh's attorney "Koskoff and McMahon." The plaintiff (Gaydosh) leaned on a fire escape railing at 1197-1209 Main Street when the railing gave way, causing Gaydosh to fall to the ground.

During the fall, Gaydosh sustained injuries to his spine, back, arms, wrists, legs, and left heel.

Gaydosh had gone to work and failed to return home; the following day, his vehicle was located near a pond.

There is no other information available about Gaydosh's disappearance.

21

Debra Lee Spickler (aka Debbie)

Missing: July 24, 1968

Vernon, Connecticut

DOB: January 22, 1955

Spickler is a 13-year-old white female, 5-05" tall, 125 pounds, with brown hair, brown eyes, a pockmark (stabbed with pencil) on her face, and a chipped tooth.

Spickler was last seen wearing a white sleeveless shirt, homemade dark green polka-dot shorts with no pockets, and white low-cut sneakers; at the time of her disappearance, Spickler lived in Mystic, Connecticut.

Spickler was visiting relatives in Vernon, Connecticut, when she was last seen at 3:30 pm walking on South Main Street near Henry Park.

A short time later, Spickler and her cousin Linda began walking on Foxhill Drive in the Henry Park swimming pool's direction when they realized they had forgotten to take bathing towels

Spickler's cousin left to return to the house to get towels, and when she returned, she could not locate Spickler; Spickler was never seen again.

(Debra Lee Spickler)

Spickler was one of seven white females who went missing in the Vernon area between 1968 and 1978.

On the same day of Spickler's disappearance, her mother received a birthday card at her home in Mystic, Connecticut, from her daughter (Debra Spickler). Debra had sent the card to her mother from her Aunt's house in Vernon, Connecticut.

The card said, "She (Debra) was being good and helping her aunt." There had been a report of a <u>strange van</u> being in the area on the day of Spickler's disappearance (Refer: Barry P.'s statement about the van).

Debra's case has several similarities with the other missing females in Vernon, Connecticut (Refer: Susan Irene and LaRosa cases).

(Refer: Susan Irene and LaRosa cases - van)

Jacqueline Winfred Kinney

Missing: December 05, 1969

Canton, Connecticut

DOB: 1934

Kinney is described as a 35-year-old white female, 5-04" tall, 150 pounds, with red hair, blue eyes, a scar on her abdomen from surgery, a scar on the left leg below the knee, a broken right toe; she was missing rear teeth, she was partial paralysis on her left side, and her left arm was partially disabled. Kinney was last seen at her residence at 7 High Street in Canton, Connecticut. Kinney was reported missing by her husband, Gerald Kinney.

In September of 1976, authorities going on a tip, dug up an old house foundation and well located inside Werner Woods State Park. The house had been damaged by a fallen tree and was torn down in 1973; inside sources would only say, "They believed someone had fallen into the well." The well had been backfilled fifteen years before the search. The search ended in September 1977; Jacqueline's husband Gerald had moved to Maine.

In 1979 the Connecticut State Police sought a warrant for a suspect (not identified) involved in Kinney's murder. It was reported the suspect once lived in Canton and knew Kinney. It was never mentioned if the suspect was ever arrested.

Irene Lanora LaRosa (aka Renee)

Missing: March 01, 1971

Ellington, Connecticut

DOB: April 10, 1953

LaRosa is a 17-year-old white female, 5-04" tall, 115 pounds, with brown hair and green eyes. LaRosa was allegedly last seen leaving her residence in Ellington, Connecticut, on March 01, 1971.

Irene was raised in the Our Lady of Rose Hill child orphanage in New Britain, Connecticut.

LaRosa was one of eleven children in the LaRosa family, taken away by state officials and relocated throughout Connecticut.

In 2016 Irene's niece Tina Richburg reported Irene missing to the Ellington police after learning that Irene's older brother Robert LaRosa (deceased) had lied to the family about filing a missing person report when Irene disappeared (1971).

Richburg said, "Things started getting weird when I started looking into things."

"My Uncle Robert wrote to me and said he filed a report in 1971 and said Irene was alive and well, and she was living in Manchester, Connecticut."

"He lied about everything and was getting very mad at me for looking into the matter."

Because Irene was not officially reported missing until 2016, it would explain why the Vernon police did not link Irene's disappearance to her brother Robert's. Robert's wife, Susan LaRosa, disappeared in 1975 (Susan's body was found in 1978).

It also explains why Irene was not included in the list of cold case disappearances and homicides in the Vernon area between 1968 and 1978.

The other disappearances included Debra Spickler, Lisa Joy White, and Janice Pockett, and the homicides of Stephanie Olisky, Susan LaRosa, Patricia Luce, and Janette Reynolds, all of which had a link to the LaRosa Family.

Several similarities began to appear during the investigation of the eight missing females in the Vernon area between 1968 and 1978. There is a possibility there may have been a different suspect in the Patricia Luce case.

In an interview conducted by the author, an ex-brother-in-law, Barry P. said he had once dated Irene; he also knew details about Susan LaRosa's murder.

Irene's two brothers, Robert (deceased) and Nathan LaRosa Jr. (deceased), are both people of interest in Irene's disappearance.

(Refer: "Susan LaRosa case" and "The LaRosa Family Interview")

Warren Joseph Niederfringer

Missing: June 01, 1972

Newington, Connecticut

DOB: 1949

Niederfringer is a 23-year-old white male, 5-09" tall, 150 pounds, with brown hair and blue eyes.

Niederfringer was last seen in Newtown, Connecticut, on June 01, 1972.

Niederfringer was last seen driving a yellow 1960's model Dodge step-van previously owned by the Connecticut Light and Power Company; he may have been traveling to Boston, Massachusetts, or North Carolina.

Janice Kathryn Pockett

Missing: July 23, 1973

Tolland, Connecticut

DOB: October 15, 1965

Pockett is a 7-year-old white female, 4-0" tall, 65 pounds, with blonde hair and blue eyes.

Pockett was last seen wearing navy blue shorts with an imprinted American flag and stars design, a blue and white pullover shirt, white socks, and blue sneakers.

Pockett's younger sister Mary Engelbrecht reported, "My sister and I were bickering," "We were driving my mom crazy, I remember," "My sister and I had been fighting over something stupid like a toothbrush, I think."

Janice asked if she could ride off alone, and her mother said, "Yes." It was a big deal, Engelbrecht said because it was the first time either girl had been allowed to go anywhere by themselves.

Pockett was last seen leaving her house on Anthony Road riding a metallic green Murray bicycle (bell and banana seat).

She left the house to search the neighborhood for a butterfly she had caught a few days earlier and had hidden under a rock.

(Reward Poster for Janice Pockett)

Pockett had an envelope to transport the butterfly back home. Her mother found Pockett's bicycle on a dirt road along Rhodes Road along an adjacent wooded area, less than a mile away from the Pockett's residence.

Neither the butterfly nor the envelope was found; it's believed the abduction occurred while Pockett was returning home. Detective Cargill reported, "The dirt road where her bike was found had tire tracks on it from various vehicles, and our investigators followed up, searching for vehicles fitting those tracks but again, no clues were found."

It was rumored that Charles Pierce, a known sexual predator and the alleged murderer, was responsible for Janice Pockett and Debra Spickler's disappearance.

Pierce claimed he had murdered as many as forty children throughout New England during the 1950s and 1970s.

Like most of Pierce's confessions and ramblings, his stories had been filled with lies and contradicting statements. In Pierce's account, he reported abducting a boy (unidentified) and then putting his body next to Pocketts body in the van. Based on Pierce's statement, he would have abducted the boy in the 1950s. However, Janice Pockett was abducted twenty-three years after the boys alleged abduction.

Police Give Up Search For Tolland Girl's Body

By MANIRA WILSON

TOLLAND — State police said Friday they were giving up their search for the remains of 7-year-old Janice Pockett unless they receive further information from a man who allegedly has confessed to her slaving.

Police had spent three days digging in a wooded area here, acting on information the man provided, but had failed to find any trace of the girl.

Police refused to identify the man they said "claimed to have intimate knowledge" of what happened to Janice, who last was seen riding her bicycle July 26, 1973.

Police also refused to comment on reports that the man, a carnival worker, had confessed to murdering the Anthony Road girl or that he recently had been arrested by Massachusetts police in a similar case there.

Police denied that the man also has confessed to the slaying of 13-year-old Debra Spickler of Mystic, contrary to earlier statements by sources close to the investigation. The Mystic teen-ager disappeared July 24, 1968, from Henry Park in the Rockville section of Vernon.

Five young females have disappeared from the area within the last 12 years.

The suspect reportedly was brought Friday morning to Old Cathole Road South, where police have been digging for Janice's body since Wednesday, to try to further pinpoint the gravesite.

The digging Friday was concentrated in a 50-foot square area near the end of the half-mile dirt road. Police earlier this week dug up smaller areas in three other spots along the isolated road.

Police said Friday night they did not plan to resume the search Monday. They would not say if they had other leads.

Old Cathole Road South is off Rhodes Road, where Janice was last seen and where her bicycle was found soon after she was reported missing about 3:30 p.m. July 26, 1973.

An intensive search by police, firefighters and volunteers soon after her disappearance had included the Old Cathole Road South property, but no trace of the girl was found.

Kathryn Pockett, Janice's mother, declined to be interviewed Friday. She said police had told the family that they would be searching, but didn't give any specifics about the man's information or any encouragement about the outcome of the search. "We just have to wait and endure," she said.

This is the second time within a year that police have searched for Janice. Last November, police spent several days diving in Walker Reservoir East in Vernon after a tip given them by a Norwich psychic. They didn't find any trace of Janice and the search was suspended because of cold weather.

(Search for Janice Pockett)

Pierce later confessed to burying Pockett's (1973) "next" to a boy (Angelo Puglisi, 1976) in an open field. Again Pierce's statement was unfounded. Based on the dates of the disappearances, Pockett had disappeared three years earlier.

Pierce said he used a spade he kept in the van to bury them; Pierce said he marked the graves with pieces of coal.

Pierce was incarcerated in 1980 for the abduction and murder of 13-year-old Michelle Wilson, who he claims he pulled into his van and strangled.

In Peirce's final jailhouse confession in 1999, three weeks before his death, the 78-year-old Pierce confessed to killing two more children in the 1940s.

Throughout Pierce's game of charades with authorities, he could never provide any creditable information in any of the cases.

Pierce reported he had buried the boy and Janice in an open field along West Street; Pierce later changed his story and said he buried Pockett along Old Cathole Road South.

Old Cathole Road South is located off Rhodes Road, where Janice disappeared.

Authorities transported Pierce from prison to Old Cathole Road South and dug a fifty-foot square grid near the end of the half-mile dirt road where Pierce reported burying Janice's body.

The authorities also dug three smaller areas along the isolated road, but no trace of Janice or the boy was ever found.

The author had discussed Pierce's confession with a detective who believed Pierce had given authorities arbitrary locations to search so he could leave the prison and spend time outside of the gate.

Pierce said he had once been employed as a carnival worker when Janice disappearance. There had been a carnival in Tolland the day after Janice's disappearance. However, the carnival records could not confirm Pierce's employment; at the time, many employees were paid under the table and kept off the records.

Like all Pierce's confessions, he could only give vague locations where he buried bodies; he could only offer "similar" names of missing children, excluding Michelle Wilson.

Peirce had a history of confessing to crimes and later recanting his stories; when asked for details of specific crimes, he would stop answering questions.

It is most probable Pierce claimed responsibility for Michelle Wilson's homicide only to prevent him from being extradited to Florida for unrelated criminal charges.

Pierce claimed he had murdered almost forty children throughout the year but could not lead authorities to any of the bodies he claimed to have killed.

(Refer to Irena and Susan LaRosa's cases and van)

(Suspect Sketch)

Billy P. and his brother Barry P. (LaRosa Interview) reported that he worked at a garage near Pockett's residence. Ann G. said her ex-husband Barry P. worked as a custodian in the Tolland school system in the early 1970s. Janice Pockett's sister told a month after her sister's disappearance, the school nurse attempted to retrieve Janice's medical records for the authorities, only to discover that Janice's files were missing.

It would be interesting to see if the school records of the other missing girls who attended the Tolland school system were also missing.

Howard W. Veillette Sr. (aka Howie)

Missing: April 01, 1974

Shelton, Connecticut

DOB: 1941

Veillette is a 32-year-old white male, 5-08" tall, 165 pounds, with brown hair, hazel eyes, and a scar on his right arm and abdomen.

Veillette was last seen in Shelton, Connecticut, on April 01, 1974.

The Connecticut State Police have Veillette listed as an Army veteran missing on April 01, 1974, but the state police have him missing from Honolulu, Hawaii.

Veillette's brother Warren died in Shelton, Connecticut, in 2015.

No other information about the case is available.

Lisa Joy White

Missing: November 01, 1974

Vernon, Connecticut

DOB: February 02, 1961

White is described as a 13-year-old white female 5-0" tall, 110 pounds, with blonde hair, blue eyes, and a scare (chickenpox) on her forehead above her right eye. White was last seen wearing green pants and a blue jean (denim) jacket.

On Halloween, the day before her disappearance, Lisa, a girlfriend, and two older boys had been driving in a car in Hampden, Massachusetts. Police stopped the vehicle for throwing a pumpkin out of a car window. Subsequently, Lisa was transported by the Hampden police back to the Connecticut State Police barrack in Tolland.

White's mother was contacted at work by the police and advised of the incident; White's mother left the job and picked up Lisa from the barracks. When Lisa disappeared, she had been grounded by her mother because of the incident involving the police the previous night.

Before sneaking out of the house, Lisa left a note for her mother, "I'm in love with an older boy, you think I'm a little girl, but I'm not."

White's sister said Lisa would hang out with older boys and men. White may have planned to meet a boyfriend that night, but this was never substantiated.

During the interview with the author, a LaRosa family member mentioned that Robert LaRosa and Nathan LaRosa, people of interest in the two LaRosa cases, had met Lisa at a party, and the LaRosas had once met lived on Ragan Road, where the LaRosas once lived.

On the night of the disappearance, White had walked two miles from her house on Regan Road to her friend's home at 108 Prospect Street (Rockville) Vernon, Connecticut.

After talking with her friend, White left the house at approximately 7:30 pm and started to walk home; an unidentified friend reported White was last seen on Oak Street.

Lisa's mother contacted the Vernon police at approximately 2:00 am on the night of the disappearance.

The Vernon police had initially considered White a runaway because she had gotten into trouble with her parents the night before and was grounded when she went missing.

Although White had threatened to run away in the past, family members reported she would only get a few houses away before returning home.

White's best friend said it would have taken two men to control her because Lisa was as strong as three people.

The author believed this statement to be true; the report further supports that more than one suspect was involved in the White's disappearances.

Although some people believe the suspect(s) in the disappearances lived outside the state, the close geographical cluster of disappearances (1968-1978) suggests otherwise.

Lisa White appears with another missing female (Patricia Luce) in a picture of the Rockville cheerleading team in the 1960s. Patricia Luce disappeared on July 18, 1978, and her remains were found on March 13, 1979, in a remote wooded area of Marlborough, Connecticut.

Many of the missing females attended the same school system, which could be a possible link.

White's stepfather reported that a female was heard screaming from a white van parked on Regan Road on the night of the disappearance. Authorities later said they believed the screaming came from an argument between a boyfriend and a girlfriend (Refer: LaRosa Family interview, soundproof van).

The complainant reported observing a man pull a female into the van and then yelling from inside the van (Refer: Barry P. interview concerning soundproof van).

Excerpt from an email from Judi (Lisa's mother) to Terry Sutton: "The other guy the state police suspected; his last name was Songailo – can't think of his first name now. I think it was Eddie.

I think he used to run a gas station on Route 30 in Vernon, and he would dump old tires and junk on the old dirt road where they found Susan LaRosa's body."

(Refer to Irene and Susan LaRosa cases – van)

Susan Sharon LaRosa

Missing - June 22, 1975 (Disappearance-Homicide)

Vernon, Connecticut

DOB: July 22, 1954

On the night of her alleged disappearance, Susan LaRosa's husband, Robert LaRosa (deceased), reported he and his wife had gotten into a verbal argument, and Susan had walked out of their second-floor apartment at 22 Ward Street, located in Vernon, Connecticut. Robert said he last saw his wife walking toward Rockville center, which was only a few blocks from their apartment.

The apartment did not have a telephone, and Susan often walked to the nearby pharmacy to call her mother on the payphone. Susan was last seen wearing a flower-patterned blouse, maroon pants, and brown loafer shoes. Richard Hyer of the Vernon police department special services unit said Susan married her husband Robert when she was 16 years old; Susan and her husband had three children.

Hyer said that they did not suspect foul play at the time of Susan's disappearance, and her husband was not a person of interest. Hyer said that there were reported sightings of Susan over the three years. Hyer noted that all the reports were investigated, but none of the sightings were substantiated.

Throughout the author's research on the case, there were four different versions of her husband's story. Robert reported 1.) "I was under the impression she took off with another guy."

"She was always flirting with guys." Susan's sister Ann G. said her sister Susan had several male friends before her disappearance.

Lieutenant Edwin Carlson (retired) reported Robert later stated 2.) "She (Susan) went out to go to the store, and she never came back."

The question was, did Susan leave with another man or go out to the store?

Susan's sister Ann G. said, "Robert was a very soft-spoken person and took a lot of shit from Susan;" this fact is later disputed during an interview with LaRosa family members.

Ann G. said if Robert had murdered Susan, it was not planned but rather a spontaneous reaction to his wife hurting one of the children.

It had been common knowledge that Susan had been physically abusive to the children in the past.

In 1978 the partial skeletal remains and pieces of clothing belonging to Susan LaRosa were found by highway workers along Route I-84 east bordering Banforth Road in Vernon, Connecticut.

The cause of death was blunt force trauma to the skull, consistent with Stacey LaRosa's statement during an interview with the author (Refer: To the Barry P. interview).

Dental records were used to identify Susan's remains. Barry P. reported observing a bloody rock on the Ward Street apartment's living room floor on the night of Susan's disappearance.

The criminal investigation into Susan's homicide did not begin until her body was found three years later. At that point, most, if not all, the forensic evidence in the second-floor Ward Street apartment had been either cleaned up or contaminated.

In 2006 samples of the apartment's wood floor were cut out and placed into evidence. However, the pieces of the wooden floor were of no evidentiary value; the story had been torn up and replaced years after Susan's homicide.

Susan's husband, Robert, and his ex-brother-in-law, Barry P., remain people of interest in Susan LaRosa's homicide. Ann G. recalled going with Robert to identify Susan's remains; she remembered Robert couldn't stop crying.

Ann G. recalls saying to Robert, "I understand if you snapped and killed Susan; it was an accident." Ann G. recalled Robert hugged her and said, "Thank you." The melancholy response seems somewhat suspicious.

I noticed in Robert's statement he never said he hadn't killed Susan. I found Ann G. overly protective of Robert.

Ann G. remembered the clothing (flower-patterned) pieces found with Susan's remains. The clothing remnant matched Susan's dress on the night of her disappearance.

John Florio described finding a putty knife wrapped in a flower-patterned piece of material hidden on top of a basement rafter in Roberts Stafford Springs apartment.

Bernette B. reported cleaning the blood off the Ward Street apartment floor and staircase with a putty knife, which Robert gave her.

Robert is also a person of interest in the 1971 disappearance and cover-up of his younger sister Irene's disappearance.

Police Await Report on Body

By KAREN MAMONE

VERNON — After nearly three years, the family of Susan LaRosa knows finally that the 20-year-old mother of three is dead.

But police, who never closed the file on the missing woman, said Monday the questions are just beginning.

Police are awaiting a medical examiner's report, on the woman whose skeleton was found Thursday by two highway workers in a wooded area south of I-86, hoping to find out how she died.

The file on Susan LaRosa was opened about 1 a.m. June 23, 1975, when her husband, Robert, then of 22 Ward St., called police and told them his wife hadn't returned after leaving the house on foot about 6:30 p.m. She had last been seen heading toward Rockville Center only a few blocks from her home.

Richard Hyer of the police special services unit, who was one of the original investigators of the disappearance, said Monday that police at the time had "no rea-

son to believe foul play was responsible." They still have no reason to believe so, he said.

Interviews at the time of her disappearance indicated that there had been problems at home, and it was reported she had argued with her husband before she left the Ward Street tenement, Hyer said.

Since the woman had married at 16½ and had three small children, Hyer said, "I

can't imagine there wouldn't have been problems."

LaRosa was never a suspect in the case, Hyer said.

As in most missing person cases, reports were received by police during the three years that Mrs. LaRosa had been sighted locally, Hyer said. All the reports were checked out, but none was substantiated.

At one point, Mrs. LaRosa's dental records were sent to Illinois to be checked

against a body found there.

It was finally those dental records, and scraps of clothing and shoes found nearby, that helped police indentify the remains found last week.

LaRosa had said his wife was wearing maroon slacks and a flowered print blouse. Bits of similar material were found at the isolated wooded site. A pair of brown loafers was found several feet away.

(Susan LaRosa's Remains Found)

(Refer to Irene LaRosa Case)

41

The LaRosa Family Interview

On Saturday, November 11, 2017, the author drove from Connecticut to Southwick, Massachusetts, to interview members of the LaRosa family to discuss the disappearance of two of their family members in the early 1970s.

In March of 1971, Irene Lenore LaRose was allegedly reported missing from her home in Ellington, Connecticut, by her older brother Robert.

In 2016 Tina Richburg, Irene's niece found out that Irene's brother Robert had lied to the family about reporting Irene missing in 1971. Robert had never reported his sister Irene missing.

Four years (1975) after Irene's disappearance, her sister-in-law Susan LaRosa, Robert's then-wife, was reported missing from her second-floor Ward Street apartment.

Robert reported to authorities the couple had been involved in a verbal argument, at which point Susan left the apartment on foot and never returned. Three years after her disappearance, Susan's remains were found by highway workers in a remote wooded area of Vernon, Connecticut, bordering Route I-84 Interstate.

I don't believe in consequences, but having two family members disappear independently in four years is suspicious enough. Having the same family member linked to both disappearances is not a consequence.

I first thought there had to be a dark family secret at play. Still, after interviewing several LaRosa family members, the truth behind Irene's disappearance and Susan's homicide had become more outlandish than I could have even imagined.

Some LaRosa family members believe two of their family members and an ex-brother-in-law were responsible for Irene's disappearance and Susan's homicide.

The LaRosa family members further believed that the two suspected family members and at least one ex-family member might have been linked to several other disappearances in the Vernon area (1968-1978).

The thought of the two suspected family members being involved in Irene's disappearance and Susan's homicide has divided the LaRosa family, with family members pointing the finger at each other.

The LaRosa family matrix is somewhat complicated. In the mid to late 1960s, the eleven LaRosa children were removed from the family home by the state department of child services and placed in either orphanages or boys' homes.

When the children grew up, they began to settle in the Ellington and Vernon area.

Ann G. (Susan LaRosa's sister) recalled that Vernon, Connecticut, in the 1960s and 1970s, was like an open Charlie Manson commune made up of child molesters, serial rapists, serial killers, and wife beaters.

The families would swap wives and children for sexual exploitation amongst other couples.

Ann G. recalls being told by family members not to walk the roads after dark. Ann G., Susan's sister (Susan LaRosa's sister), recalled her parents telling her not to walk the streets in the darkness and stay away from the LaRosa house.

According to some LaRosa family members, the primary person of interest in Irene LaRosa's disappearance was her 29-year-old brother Nunzio S. LaRosa Jr. (aka Nathan) (deceased, 1998).

43

Before moving to Ellington, Connecticut, Nathan and his brother Robert (deceased, 2018) lived together in a boy's home; according to family members, the brothers had a tighter-than-glue relationship (You lie, and I'll swear to it).

Family members recalled early in life. Nathan was a known child molester with a violent temper. Nathan's younger brother Rudy told the author his brother Nathan had severe mental and anger issues "You could tell by just looking at him, he wasn't right."

Several family members recalled Nathan molesting all the female family members and females living in the local area.

Family members considered Nathan too dangerous to live in the family house with the children, so they made him live in a trailer in the backyard.

In the late 1960s, Nathan had resided on Regan Road, the same road where Lisa White had lived.

The original LaRosa house (now raised) was located at Pine Street and Wendell Road in Ellington, Connecticut.

Richburg recalled a covered well-house on the property referred to by the family as the "rape fort," this is where Nathan would take the girls to molest them.

Rudy said the well-house the family members were referred to as the "rape fort" was not in the location that the family described.

Rudy said the well-house was a kid's fort, and Nathan was too fat (256 pounds) to fit inside.

Rudy recalled when the camper behind the house became dilapidated, his parents had it removed from the property.

Nathan began living in a shed on the adjacent property across from the house; this structure was where Nathan would take the girls.

At the time, Rudy said he noticed a possible relationship between Irene, 17, and Nathan, 29.

On a few occasions, Rudy observed Irene sneaking down to the camper. Debbie (Irene's sister) said a well-to-do family who knew the LaRosas had given dresses to the LaRosa girls, and the dresses were stored in Nathan's camper; this was why Irene started going down to the trailer.

2 Accused Of Assault On 2 Sons

VERNON — A Stafford couple was arraigned in Common Pleas Court 19 here Friday on charges stemming from the alleged sexual assault of their two minor children.

Nunzio LaRosa Jr., 33, and his wife, Marjorie LaRosa, 40, of Handel Road, were arrested Thursday night on Common Pleas Court 19 warrants and were held overnight in lieu of bond for their court appearance, police said.

LaRosa was charged with two counts of second-degree sexual assault and two counts of injury or risk of injury to a minor. Mrs. LaRosa was charged with one count of injury or risk of injury in connection with the alleged assault of her 12-and 15-year-old sons, police said.

Police said LaRosa allegedly assaulted his stepsons while Mrs. LaRosa was present.

The boys have been placed with the state Department of Social Services as wards for 30 days, Common Pleas Court Prosecutor Arthur P. Meisler said.

Judge Harry Hammer contined the cases to Wednesday. LaRosa is free on a $10,000 surety bond. Mrs. LaRosa is free on a $1,000 surety bond.

(Nathan LaRosa Arrested)

Rudy said Irene would go to the camper with her sister, and Nathan would chase them away and only allow Irene to stay; he believed it was at this point that Nathan began molesting Irene.

A family member said Irene was dating a math teacher (not confirmed) from Enfield named "Bob."

It was reported that Irene had run away and was living with the teacher, but the teacher had convinced Irene to move back home, and he wanted to meet her parents.

Debbie L. said, "Irene fell hard and loved the teacher."

Most family members believe the story about the teacher was a cover-up to protect other family members involved in Irene's disappearance.

It is more probable that Irene told either Robert or Nathan she would report the sexual abuse to the authorities, and at this point, she was murdered.

Family members believed that Nathan's brother Robert lied about filing a missing person's report for Irene to protect Nathan or himself.

Family members believe that when Nathan was in the boy's home, he was molested, which in turn caused his violent behavior and perverse sexual tendencies. When Nathan came home (Ellington) from the boy's home, his mother did not want anything to do with him, so his father let him live in the camper in the backyard.

Before moving to Ellington in 1968, both Robert and Nathan lived in Tolland, Vernon, and Enfield in the areas of all the disappearances.

When Nathan's father died in 1970, Nathan took control of the household; and began molesting all the females in the house. Three weeks after his father's death, Nathan's mother met another man (Frank Davis) (deceased) who moved into the main house in Ellington, and once again, Nathan was pushed to the side and sent back to live in the backyard.

46

Man Faints at Sentencing

VERNON — A 34-year-old Ellington man, sentenced to a three-to-eight-year prison term Thursday on charges of sexual assault and risk of injury to a minor, apparently passed out in his chair in Tolland County Superior Court at the time of sentencing and was brought to Rockville General Hospital when attempts to revive him failed.

Nunzio S. LaRosa Jr. of 266 Sandy Beach Road was treated and released to authorities, a hospital spokeswoman said.

LaRosa, whose attorney had argued for a period of strictly supervised probation rather than imprisonment to help a "psychologically fragile" man, received a two-to-

four-year term on two counts of injury or risk of injury to a minor and a count of second-degree sexual assault, plus a consecutive one-to-four-year term on a second charge of second-degree sexual assault.

Authorities said the charges stem from assaults on two juvenile boys.

Atty. David M. Borden, who referred to psychiatric reports identifying LaRosa as suicidal, schizophrenic and paranoid, quickly asked Judge Walter J. Sidor for a recess when he realized that LaRosa, sitting beside him, wasn't responding.

The courtroom was cleared as attempts to revive LaRosa failed and ambulance attendants arrived to transport him to the hos-

pital.

Burglary

In another matter, three men pleaded guilty to third-degree burglary and second-degree larceny in an Oct. 2 break into a home on Munson Road in Stafford.

Pleading guilty were Joseph Kaminsky, 21, of Ellington Road, East Hartford; William D. Herrera, 19, of Oakland Street, Manchester; and Alan R. Muldoon, 20, of Rachel Road, Manchester.

Assistant State's Atty. Abbot B. Schwebel said the three broke into the home through a rear door, ransacked the home and stole $1,100 worth of goods.

The men will be sentenced Jan. 4.

(Nathan LaRosa Sentencing)

Nathan's younger brother Rudy said Nathan was violent; Debbie L. recalled that people in the family did whatever Nathan wanted out of fear. While serving in the military, it was reported that Nathan attempted to kill his commanding officer, and he had spent time in a mental institution.

It was a well-known fact that Nathan and his brother Robert were both hunters and owned guns; it was also a well-known fact that Nathan would kill animals, including family pets (Jeffery Dahmer Syndrome).

Debbie L. recalled when Nathan lived with them on Regan Road, he came into the house and asked her, "What's wrong with your dog?" Debbie L. said when she went outside, she found her dog lying at the bottom of the stairs, and the dog's body was still warm.

47

Debbie L. recalled that Nathan would stand outside the house watching the children playing on the street. A family member reported it Nathan might have met Lisa White at a party. However, this fact could not be confirmed.

Nathan had also been involved in the search for Janice Pockett, which explains why he was involved in the search.

Could Nathan have been interested in what the searchers and authorities said about crime?

LaRosa's family members reported that Nathan, Robert, Barry P., and Billy P. worked at a garage in the area where Janice lived.

Rudy said he was arguing with his mother one day, and his mother told Nathan to beat him up. Rudy said, "When Nathan started to lose the fight, Nathan grabbed a piece of ground cable and attempted to strangle me."

Family members described Nathan as "Pure evil."

When her grandmother and her new boyfriend (Frank Davis) moved to Florida in 1980, Richburg said Nathan went with them; this was when Vernon's disappearances and the surrounding areas stopped.

Richburg recalls that when she was 11 years old, she had driven with her father Rudy to Florida to visit Nathan. On the trip to Florida, my father told the kids not to go near Nathan. When we arrived in Florida, my father told Nathan not to look or talk to the children.

When Nathan was on his death bed in Rockville General Hospital, Richburg said he kept telling his older sister Claudette he had something to confess to her.

Some family members believe he wanted to confess to Claudette that he had murdered Irene. Others believe Nathan wanted to apologize for molesting her.

A confession involves a crime. An apology is asking for forgiveness. As fate would have it, when Nathan told Claudette he wanted to confess something to her, Claudette abruptly walked out of the hospital room. Nathan LaRosa died of congestive heart failure before making his confession.

Nathan married his first wife, Bertha Porter-LaRosa (06/19/65) (status unknown), divorced. Nathan married his second wife, Marjorie LaRosa (06/1972) (deceased); Nathan had no children from either marriage.

Nathan had been incarcerated from (01/16/1976 – 01/20/1976) and (11/18/1976 – 01/29/1979) for raping his two stepsons. This excluded Nathan from being a suspect in the Patricia Luce (07/18/1978) and Janette Reynolds (08/27/1978) homicides (Refer: Person of Interest).

Richburg recalled Robert and Nathan might have met another victim Kathleen Terry at one of their summer camps at either Mashapaug (Union, Connecticut) or Hammonasset (Madison, Connecticut) state park. Kathleen Terry was a 12-year-old female who was abducted and murdered on July 19, 1974, while riding her bike in a remote wooded area in Sturbridge, Massachusetts; this case was similar to the Pockett case. The alleged serial killer Charles Pierce eventually confessed to the homicide

It was later believed Pierce had lied about Terry's murder to prevent his extradition to Florida for other criminal offenses.

Richburg said she contacted the Connecticut State Police task force and provided them with the information she had found out about the suspected family members and their possible link to the other disappearances.

She also provided the locations of the old LaRosa property in Ellington, where evidence might be found. Richburg told the author that while excavating several wells on the old LaRosa property and adjacent properties in Ellington, pieces of children's clothing were found in one of the wells.

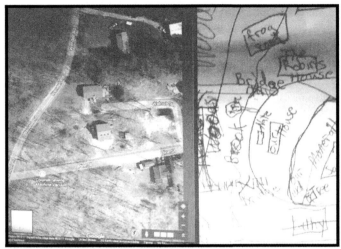

(Old LaRosa property- Hand-drawn map of property)

The author had spoken with a state trooper who investigated the case. I was told there were several summer camps in the area, the wells had become a community dumping ground, and garbage was found everywhere and in the wells.

The wells were filled with garbage, including car parts and children's clothing. However, none of the clothing pieces belonged to any children who had disappeared in the area.

The Susan LaRosa Homicide

Over time many stories about the Susan LaRosa case have been told. Still, when the author interviewed Stacey LaRosa (Susan LaRosa's daughter), her facial expression and reaction to specific questions told me she had witnessed something extremely traumatizing as a child.

Stacey recalled that she was three years old when her mother's homicide occurred. Stacey said she had witnessed her mother's murder on the second-floor Ward Street apartment on June 22, 1975.

Stacey said we were all in the living room, and my mother changed my younger brother Maurice's diaper. My other brother Robert Jr. pulled my hair, and I began to cry.

My mother (Susan) slapped my brother in the face causing his nose to bleed. My father, Robert, was working with pieces of metal in the kitchen.

When my mother hit my brother in the face, my father ran out of the kitchen with something in his hand and hit my mother in the head. During the interview with Barry P., it was later determined that the object used in the homicide was a rock.

My mother fell to the floor and did not move. I saw a large pool of dark blood on the living room floor around my mother's head. My father told me, "My mother was sleeping."

The state medical examiner's report indicated Susan LaRosa had died from a localized blunt force trauma to the head.

Existing child service reports indicate Susan had hurt the children in the past. However, the author will not discuss the graphic nature of the events.

Stacey reported, "While my mother was lying on the floor, my father left the apartment; a short time later, he came back with another man I believed to be Barry P."

Stacey recalled the other man was wearing a red and black flannel shirt and smelt like cherry pipe tobacco.

During my interview with Ann G., she confirmed her ex-husband Barry smoked Captain's Black Cherry tobacco in his pipe.

At the time of the murder, Barry P. lived around the corner from LaRosa's apartment.

My father and the man carried my mother down the second-floor staircase and put my mother into my father's dark brown Chevrolet Caprice.

Robert's ex-sister-in-law Bernette B. told the author she used a putty knife to scrape the blood off the floor and staircase the following day.

During the interview with Barry P., he placed himself and his ex-wife at the Ward Street apartment just after the murder. However, his ex-wife Ann G. failed to mention that fact to me during my interview with her.

Family members said Susan had a history of abusing the children and her husband. Family members believed that if Susan had hurt one of the children, Robert might have unintentionally reacted out of rage.

Robert may have acted out of rage in this case, but what about Irene's case? Why had he lied to the family about filing a missing person report?

Robert's new girlfriend, Robin S., had started to move her clothes into the Ward Street apartment before Susan's murder.

It wasn't until Susan's body was found three years later (1978) that an official criminal investigation into the murder began. Still, by then, all of the biological evidence was cleaned from the apartment and staircase.

When authorities attempted to locate Robert's Chevrolet-Capri (suspect vehicle), they could not find it. Barry P. later confirmed the Chevrolet-Capri did have Susan's body in it.

Robert told the authorities he had sold the car but couldn't remember the buyer's name. The police never located the vehicle, and the car was never re-registered. Barry P's dark blue AMC-Rambler mysteriously disappeared and was never re-registered (Jenette Reynolds case).

I don't believe in coincidences. At the time, Robert and Berry P. were both related and working at the same salvage yard located on Shaker Road in Enfield, Connecticut. The vehicles were probably salvaged (crushed) to destroy evidence.

After her mother's body was brought to the car, Stacey recalled that her father returned to the apartment and then went to the hospital. So, who dumped Susan's body? Ann G. said on the night of Susan's alleged disappearance, her ex-husband Berry P. did not return home until the following day.

Ann G. accompanied Robert when he went to identify Susan's remains. Ann G. said she understood if Robert acted out of anger when she told Robert. All Robert said was, "Thank you." Susan was wearing a flower-patterned dress. The putty knife was wrapped in a flowery pattern fabric.

During my interview with Barry P., he placed himself at the crime scene; he described the crime scene and knew Susan's body was in the car. He told the author about the murder weapon and that his ex-wife was present at the Ward Street apartment on the night of the homicide. During my interview with Ann G., she failed to mention any of the information provided by Barry.

Ann G. told the author that after Susan's disappearance, when she would get into a fight with her ex-husband Barry, he would slap her and say, "The next time, the same thing that happened to your sister will happen to you."

The day after Susan's disappearance, Robert asked Bernette B., Susan's younger 14-year-old sister, to clean the blood off the floor.

The author asked Bernette B. how she cleaned the blood off the floor and staircase. Bernette said Robert gave her a <u>putty knife</u> to scrape the dried (congealed) blood off the floor; Barry later confirmed this during our interview.

Bernette B. said the blood she cleaned was on the floor in the living room several feet away from the kitchen, and there was a blood trail leading from the second floor down the stairs to the outside door of the building.

Bernette B. said Robert told her the blood was from his son's bloody nose. Bernette B. said she knew Robert was lying because there was too much blood on the floor and a blood trail leading down the staircase.

Bernette B. recalled that Robert took the putty knife back after using the putty knife to scrape the blood off the floor.

She said she did not know what happened to the putty knife after Robert had taken it; Bernette B. was the second witness to the crime scene. Bernette B. said she babysat Susan's children all summer in the Ward Street apartment after Susan's disappearance.

Bernette B. recalled that four days after Susan had disappeared, Robert's new girlfriend, Robin S. (now wife), moved into the Ward Street apartment.

Bernette B. recalled that the apartment was sweltering during the summer, and there were several fans in the windows. She recalled that she asked Robert if she could have a fan for her room, and he said, "No, but you can come and stay in my room with me."

Bernette B. said that at the end of the summer, Robert's daughter Stacey had moved out of the house and in with her godparents, Philip (deceased) and Cheryl Isham. Bernette said she slept over at her godparent's house the first night Stacey stayed there.

She recalled Stacey had fallen asleep, and at some point during the night, Stacey woke up and began screaming, "My father hit my mother in the head, and she won't wake up."

Bernette said this had occurred several times over the next few months. Stacey said she told her godparents about seeing her father kill her mother; her godparents brought her to the Vernon police department to give a statement.

Stacey believes the authorities did not believe her story because she was a young child at the time of the incident.

It is also possible because of the history of prior domestic violence complaints at LaRosa's Ward Street apartment, the police may have shrugged the disappearance off until Susan's body was found three years later.

All of the statements made by Stacey were collaborated by other witnesses.

Debbie L. Robert (younger sister) said she was the person who cleaned a tiny blood smear on the wall, but the blood was from the son being struck by Susan. During our conversation, I felt Debbie L. was being deceptive and covering for Robert.

Remember Bernette B.'s story about cleaning up the blood and watching Robert's children that summer was collaborated by Berry P.

During the interviews with Ann G. and Debbie L., they were attempting to protect Robert. Stacey said she began asking questions about her mother's murder when she was young.

She remembers her father, Robert, and his new wife, Robin S. becoming furious when she started asking her mother questions. In turn, Robert brought Stacey to a doctor, and her father requested the doctor to prescribe Stacey psychotherapeutic (mind-altering) medication.

Stacey reported that family members had told her that her memories of the incident (Susan's homicide) were suggested to her by other family members when she was young.

There was no doubt that what Stacey saw in the apartment that night traumatized her even into adulthood. Again, all of the information provided to the author by Stacey was collaborated by other people the author interviewed.

I contacted a psychologist and posed two questions, 1.) Could a 3-year-old child remember traumatic events as clearly as Stacey described? And 2.) Could family members, by suggestion, brainwash her into believing she saw her father murder her mother?

The psychologist answered, 1.) "Yes, it is common for young children to remember traumatic events clearly," and 2.) "No, people cannot simply be brainwashed or cause post-traumatic stress syndrome to another person by suggesting a scripted story."

Stacey said her father had her institutionalized several times when she began asking questions about her mother.

She said that when she was 12 years old, she began asking questions about her mother's murder. Stacey said she was put in the family car by her father and his new wife and abandoned on Marshall Street in Hartford, Connecticut. Stacey said, "It was a better option than what happened to my mother."

Several years after Susan's disappearance, Robert and his wife, Robin S., moved to an apartment in Stafford Springs. While living in the apartment, their daughter Roberta (deceased) began dating the next-door neighbor, John "Pyle" Florio (deceased).

Family members reported that at the time, there was no love loss between John Florio and his girlfriend's parents, Robert and Robin. After Roberta's death at 25, Florio moved in with Stacey and her husband.

Stacey recalled during a conversation with Florio, Florio told Stacey and her husband that before Roberta's death, he was in the basement of the Stafford Springs apartment looking around when he found a cigar box hidden on top of the basement rafters.

Florio told Stacey and her husband; that the cigar box contained a bloody putty knife wrapped in a flower-patterned piece (Susan's dress) of fabric.

Stacey said she was surprised when Florio told her about the cigar box and the putty knife because she said she never knew about the putty knife until Florio told her. When I (author) told Barry P. that Florio had found the putty knife, he stopped in mid-sentence and said, "Really."

Stacey said when she began asking questions about the putty knife, she was told by Bernette B. that she had used a putty knife to clean the blood off the Ward Street apartment floor and staircase the day after Susan's disappearance.

During the author's interviews with LaRosa family members, three family members knew about the putty knife, and two of these family members had direct contact with the putty knife.

It is believed that Florio may have overheard a conversation between Robert and Robin concerning the putty knife. Then, Florio began snooping around in the basement, and by chance, he had found the cigar box containing the putty knife.

The Vernon police initially denied any knowledge of the putty knife; however, Barry P. said Robert had members of the police department in his back pocket and believed the police destroyed the evidence.

During my interview with witnesses, several individuals identified and confirmed the putty knife's existence as part of the crime. So we know the putty knife did exist, so where is it? Several LaRosa family members knew it was used to clean up blood from the Ward Street apartment.

Based on Barry's statement and his response when I told him the putty knife was found, my gut instinct tells me the putty knife did exist.

On November 13, 2006, John Florio received a letter from the Vernon police department's detective bureau thanking him for assisting in the Susan LaRosa case. Still, the letter did not elaborate on the extent of Florio's assistance in the case.

The author reviewed the letter given to Florio by the Vernon police; it did not indicate what type of evidence Florio turned in, but I wouldn't expect it. In 2006 John Florio began cooperating with the Vernon police concerning Susan LaRosa's homicide. He later died under suspicious circumstances in 2008 at 43.

The author spoke with a Connecticut State Police Task Force member about the letter sent to John Florio; the task force member said he did know a letter was given to Florio by the Vernon police department. The CSP indicated that the letter was merely a thank you jester to Florio for cooperating in the investigation.

I believe Florio did find and turn over the putty knife to the Vernon police department. I know the task force member I spoke with gave me a line of shit about the letter.

Still, I got Barry P. to tell me what happened the night of the murder, and again the putty knife was brought up during the conversation. Interestingly, when the Vernon police found out Stacey had the original copy of the letter given to Florio, they wanted it back.

In 2002, twenty-seven years after the homicide, authorities returned to the Ward Street apartment and removed sections of the floor in hopes of recovering forensic evidence.

It had been reported that trace amounts of biological materials were recovered; however, due to limited DNA capabilities at the time, authorities could not identify any specific donor (Hamilton, 2002).

The authorities hadn't returned to the apartment until 2002, but the building had been completely renovated decades earlier.

During the author's interview with LaRosa family members, it was apparent that individual family members omitted information to protect other family members. They may have been frightened of other family members with Mafia ties, or they might not have wanted to bring embarrassment to the family, but still, waters run deep.

In one interview, the author got too close to the fire, and strange things began to happen.

I interviewed LaRosa family members for about a month when, early one Sunday morning, my cell phone started getting strange text messages from Ann G. and Terri S., both of Susan's sisters I had previously interviewed.

The interview with the two ex-family members added additional information that incriminated two of the primary people of interest in Susan's homicide and Irene's disappearance.

The text messages occurred within minutes and suggested I was lying about information. This was an interesting statement considering the only information I was given during interviews came from family members, so who was lying?

I believe they realized they had given me damaging information about the two people of interest and got scared, so they ended their communications with me.

I later found the two LaRosa family members who had bombarded me with the texts and contacted Lisa White's sister and gave erroneous information to her so she wouldn't talk to me.

Maybe they had figured out that I had found the link between Susan's homicide and Irene's disappearance, which involved one or two of their family members. It made me ask the question; what hiding from me? The interviews also suggested that Lisa White could have been an acquaintance of one of the LaRosa family members suspected in the disappearances.

During my interview with the two ex-family members, they provided disturbing information about Susan's personal life. Still, the discussions helped me understand the family dynamics during the disappearances.

The author declined to print the information about Susan in the book. The second text message said I was merely interviewing people to write a book.

Let's get this straight; first and foremost, the main objective was to identify people interested in the LaRosa cases and find possible links to other disappearances in the Vernon area, not sell books.

On the other hand, at least I don't lie about the facts about people who have gone missing or were murdered.

The book would have been written with or without their help, regardless of the fact.

In March 2018, it became clear it was time to call Robert LaRosa and Barry P. and ask them questions about the cases.

Barry P. was the only family member with enough balls to tell me what happened at the Ward Street apartment on the night of the homicide, although he failed to include his involvement in the crime; he wasn't involved in Susan's homicide, so I let it slide.

The interview was compelling, and it answered many questions I had about the two LaRosa cases. I believe Barry P's part was motivated merely out of fear of Robert LaRosa.

Unfortunately, the author didn't get the opportunity to interview Robert; he died in North Carolina a few days before I made the telephone call.

A Conversation with Barry P.

Barry P. said that on June 22, 1975, he was made aware of a problem at the LaRosa apartment on Ward Street (Robert had left the apartment and went to get Barry). Barry said when he and his wife approached the building, he saw Robert watching them through the window (During my interview with Ann G., she failed to tell me she was with her husband Barry at the apartment that night).

Barry said, Robert, meet him at the front door of the building and began yelling, "Stay away from my fucking car," "Get the fuck away from the car." I asked Barry why Robert didn't want you near his car; Barry replied, "Because Susan's body was in it." Stacey saw her father and the other man carry Susan's body to the vehicle.

When he went into the apartment, Barry said, "The apartment looked like a battlefield." Barry said the apartment was covered in blood. "It looked like someone tore the head off of a cat and swung it around the apartment by its tail; blood was all over the floor and on the wall."

Barry said. What caught his attention was a blood-covered rock lying on the living room floor. I never told Barry that Susan was struck in the head, nor did I tell him the murder occurred in the living room.

Barry said Robert told him that Susan had hurt one of the kids. Barry said he met Robert at the hospital where the boy had been taken later that night.

Barry said Robert told him Susan had left the hospital and was walking home. Robert told Barry he saw Susan get into a car while walking on the road. Barry said he knew Robert was lying about Susan getting into a car because you couldn't see the road from the hospital window.

Barry said Susan was always skittish about getting into other people's cars. Barry asked Robert how he saw Susan get into a car from the hospital window; Robert said, "Don't worry about it." The story was merely an alibi to fill up the timeline while Susan's body was being dumped.

Barry said the next day, and his ex-sister-in-law Bernette B. scraped the dry blood off the floor with a putty knife.

Barry stated that Bernette B. was the person who cleaned the blood off the apartment floor and staircase, not Debbie L., and Bernette was the person who watched the LaRosa children that summer, not Debbie L.

Barry recalled Robert's new girlfriend, Robin moving her clothes into the Ward Street apartment days before Susan was murdered. (This brings to question whether the homicide resulted from rage or premeditated)?

I asked Barry who he thought murdered Susan; he said her husband without hesitation. Barry believes Robert's brother Nathan could be the other person Stacey saw in the apartment that night. However, Nathan did not fit the physical description of the person Stacey saw in the apartment that night.

Barry was the one in the apartment that night; Nathan was Barry's brother-in-law, so Barry would have known if it was Nathan he saw in the apartment that night.

Even if the police knew Robert killed Susan, Barry said it was unlikely they would have charged him. Barry said Robert had the whole police department in his back pocket.

It was known around town that if you got into trouble, you called Robert, and by the next day, the problem had disappeared.

Barry recalls being a passenger in a car that Robert was driving, and Robert was exceptionally drunk and driving on both sides of the road. The local police stopped Robert. The police officer walked up to the car window and spoke with Robert. The police officer said, "Okay, Rob," the police officer got back into his patrol car and left.

When I asked Barry if he thought either Robert or Nathan were involved in the other girl's disappearances in the Vernon area, he thought about it and said, "I wouldn't doubt it."

Barry said he remembered Robert buying an old van-style ambulance. Robert asked me to do some wiring in the van.

Barry said he noticed the van was soundproofed, so he asked Robert why he had soundproofed the van, and Robert replied, "Because I can put whoever I wanted in the back of the van and do whatever I wanted."

The KidMissing podcast interviewed the author about the disappearance of Irene and Susan LaRosa. The link to the podcast is listed at the bottom of the page.

http://www.blogtalkradio.com/kidmissing/2018/02/10/irene-and-susan-larosa.

Stephanie Bettie Olisky

Missing: July 21, 1975 (Homicide Undetermined)

East Windsor, Connecticut

DOB: 1960

On July 21, 1975, Stephanie Olisky, 15, had left a party at a friend's house in nearby Warehouse Point (East Windsor).

She left her friend's party to return to her home on Prospect Hill Road. A motorist found Olisky lying unconscious on Route 5 between the East Winsor Grille and Claude's Gulf gas station near the Route I-91 Bridge Street underpass.

Olisky died on Friday at 7:05 am at the Mount Sinai Hospital in Hartford due to her injuries.

Chief Olmstead said the area of Route #5 where Olisky was found was beyond her home; she may have been driven there.

Chief Gerald Olmsted said the police were working on the case.

Olmsted said rumors about Olisky being struck in the head with a blunt object weren't correct, "This isn't true," Olmsted said, adding there were no witnesses to the incident (Hartford Courant, August 02, 1975).

65

An autopsy confirmed that Olisky's death resulted from a skull fracture, which could have resulted from a fall. The girl had hit her head in some undetermined manner (Hartford Courant, August 08, 1975).

Police reported, "The town was just too small at the time for somebody not to know what happened," "It's just a very well-kept secret."

The Vernon Creeper

Some people believed the disappearances and homicides of females in the Vernon area between 1968 -1978 were committed by an individual(s) living outside the state.

If the reader considers the location of each crime, you will notice they all fall within a limited geographical area.

It was previously believed two possible persons of interest lived in the bordering State of Massachusetts; however, the disappearances and homicide dump sites suggested otherwise.

Charles Pierce, who resided in Massachusetts at the time of the disappearances, claimed responsibility for over fifty murders; however, he could not lead authorities to any of the bodies he allegedly murdered.

Pierce was incarcerated because he confessed to murdering Michelle Wilson. The authorities unofficially believed that Pierce had admitted to murdering Wilson only to stop him from being extradited to Florida on unrelated charges.

Serial killers will often stay on the main roads to prevent getting lost while trying to flee the scene. The suspect will often dump their victims along main roads, not venturing far from their vehicle.

The disappearances and murders occurred in a limited local geographical area where the suspect(s) were familiar and felt safe. Other similarities in the Vernon cases are that some of the bodies were caused by blunt trauma to the head. This should not be considered a coincidental occurrence, as some believe, but rather a consistent pattern of Modus of Operandi.

In each of these cases, the suspect takes a several month cooling-of-period; this is a typical pattern among serial killers because they believe the cooling-off period creates a distance between themselves and their victims. It also indicates that the killer's motive was more psychological than materialistic.

To the public, the Vernon suspect(s) would have displayed antisocial characteristics, including a history of police contacts for crimes of violence; the suspect would have acted impulsively and would have the capability of being a skillful liar.

This type of disorder would have begun to appear during the suspect's teenage years and continues into adulthood; as an adult, the suspect would have lacked the desire to work, nor would they have had the ability to stay employed for an extended time.

This type of psychological disorder often manifests itself at an early age; in most cases, the individual was sexually or physically abused at a young age.

The suspect's family structure would have consisted of parents suffering from alcohol or substance abuse problems.

The disorder often manifests itself in families with a history of psychological problems; childhood traumas are crucial in the serial killer's behavioral patterns.

This psychological condition would have extended beyond antisocialism. It would be considered a psychopathic disorder as the individual feels no remorse or guilt, only personal gratification for their crimes. These individuals display symptoms of paranoia or suspicious (stalking/creeper) behavior.

The victims were all white females between the ages of 7 to 20; the younger victims disappeared, and their bodies were never found before 1975. The bodies had been hidden.

After 1975 the bodies of the older victims were found dumped along the road suggesting a different killer or a need to change the Modus of Operandi. The question becomes, what caused the shift in killers inhabits?

Person of Interest

The author believes the people of interest in the two LaRosa cases were possibly involved in other disappearances in Vernon and bordering towns in the late 1960s and 1970s. However, another individual, Raymond Slater (deceased) of Chaplin, Connecticut, had become another person of interest in the latter cases (1975-1978).

Slater's criminal Modus of Operandi parallels known facts surrounding the Stephanie Olisky, Patricia Luce, and Jeanette Reynolds cases.

Slater's criminal history of sexual crimes began in 1965 and continued until 1979.

Slater would find his victims walking along the road. He was known to use a weapon when abducting the victim. He also removed the victim from the crime scene. The crimes were all sexually motivated; his victims were dumped from the vehicle and left along the road.

Man Pleads Guilty to Restraint

VERNON — A 29-year-old Hartford Turnpike man pleaded guilty Thursday in Tolland County Superior Court to first-degree unlawful restraint in connection with a Nov. 22, 1976 incident in which he used a flashing blue light to stop a woman motorist on Bolton Road.

Entering the plea before Judge John F. Shea Jr. was Roland Slater Jr., a volunteer fireman at the time of the incident. Slater, who is free on a $5,000 bond, will be sentenced April 21.

State's Atty. Donald B. Caldwell said Slater was following a woman motorist in his car at about 10 p.m., when he used a flashing blue light to pull her car to the side of Bolton Road. Once both vehicles were stopped, Caldwell said, Slater pointed a gun at the woman and told her to turn off the headlights. The gun was identified as a BB pistol.

The woman refused to submit to Slater's demands, Caldwell said, and Slater fled as the woman tried to alert a passing vehicle.

Caldwell said he has agreed with the defense to submit the matter for sentencing without a recommendation, but said he reserves the right to suggest that Slater should serve a prison term for the crime.

Caldwell didn't prosecute a reckless endangerment charge against Slater.

In another matter, a 26-year-old East Hartford man pleaded guilty in Superior Court to multiple burglary and larceny counts.

Byron H. Shields of 72 Saunders St. entered the pleas on three counts of second-degree larceny, one count of third-degree larceny and two counts of second-degree burglary.

Caldwell said the charges include two breaks at a Willington home in November and December 1976 and the theft of a van in Florida. The van was driven to Connecticut by Shields and a companion.

The charges also include a break at a Stone House Road, Stafford, home. Caldwell said Shields and his companion broke into the home Dec. 20, 1976 and occupied the home until Dec. 25, removing goods valued at about $600.

71

Man, 20, Charged In Assault

CHAPLIN (Special) — Roland W. Slater Jr., 20. of North Bear Hill Road, was charged Monday with assault to commit rape and carrying a dangerous weapon.

State police arrested Slater at 1 p.m. after an incident at Diana's Pool on Rt. 198.

Police allege Slater struck his victim — a young unidentified West Hartford girl — in the head with the butt of a pistol.

Slater was held overnight in Brooklyn State Jail on $2,500 bond for Circuit Court 11 appearance today in Willimantic.

Family members and friends were among others who hindered many of these cases.

In some cases, family members knew their relatives were involved in the disappearances or homicides, but they failed to contact the authorities and lied to protect family members.

During my interview with several of the LaRosa family members, it was apparent that several members believed that a LaRosa family member had murdered their victims or had hidden or destroyed evidence in some of the cases. Yet, they still failed to report the information to the authorities.

72

Jane Doe (East Haven, Connecticut)

Found: August 16, 1975

93UFCT (Doe Network)

East Haven, Connecticut

On August 16, 1975, an unidentified white female estimated to be 18 to 29 years old, 5-06" tall, 125 pounds, with brown hair, hazel eyes, a mole under her chin, possible nose surgery, and braces was found in a drainage ditch by a truck driver.

The victim was wrapped in a tarp and found floating in a drainage ditch behind the former Bradlees department store on Frontage Road in East Haven, Connecticut.

The victim was wrapped in a tarp; paint drops were found on the tarp leading investigators to believe her killer may have been a painter.

The victim had died four to five days before her body was discovered.

The victim was bound and gagged with a black antenna wire around her neck, waist, and knees. None of her clothing was found. It was determined that she died of strangulation. Her identity is still unknown, and the case is unsolved.

Maria Florence Anjiras (aka Mia)

Missing: February 12, 1976

Norwalk, Connecticut

DOB: August 10, 1961

Anjiras is a 14-year-old white female, 5-06" tall, 120 pounds, with brown hair and blue eyes. Anjiras was a freshman at Norwalk High School and was last seen wearing a Norwalk High School jacket with the words "Mia" and the number "79" on the coat's back.

Anjiras was last seen leaving her home at 2 Milwood Road on a blue English racing bicycle. Anjiras's father later found her bicycle at her best friend's house at 50 Mary's Lane, approximately one mile from Maria's home.

Two weeks before the disappearance, Anjiras had threatened to run away from home because of a stranded relationship with her father (Constance Anjiras). Maria Anjiras had told a childhood friend that her father was overprotective.

On the day of her disappearance, neighbors reported Maria yelling, "I'm leaving and never coming back!"

Anjiras's parents denied that the altercation had taken place. When she left the house, her parents reported she had taken several sweaters, a pair of jeans, pajamas, and money.

Anjiras was last seen by her father on February 12, 1976, at approximately 2:15 pm at their home before leaving for work. Anjiras was supposed to attend a vocal lesson before babysitting a neighbor's child at 5:00 pm.

When Anjiras failed to attend both appointments, her father contacted the Norwalk police at 5:45 pm and reported her missing.

Anjiras's parents and friends reported getting unusual phone calls after her disappearance. When they picked the phone up, the caller would hang up without saying anything.

Months after her disappearance, Anjiras was sighted in close vicinity to her home by several people who knew her.

A teacher at Norwalk High School reported seeing Anjiras at the Duchess Restaurant on Main Street in Norwalk.

Over a short period, there had been other sightings of Anjiras near the Duchess Restaurant in Norwalk. She was said to have been a passenger in an orange and black vehicle.

In August of 1976, Anjiras was seen by a classmate at the Safari Pub on Westport Avenue in Norwalk, Connecticut.

The classmate reported she had told Anjiras, "She should go home," the classmate reported Anjiras was crying and said, "I know." The classmate said Anjiras was with a man who was a known Charter Oaks Motorcycle club member.

The reported sighting was never verified, but the report is believed to be valid because the biker's information (known to police) was accurate.

At the time of the disappearance, the Charter Oaks Motorcycle clubhouse was located on Woodward Avenue in Norwalk.

However, after the Norwalk police raided the clubhouse in 1972, the club moved to Greenwood Avenue in Bethel, Connecticut.

The Norwalk police had advised the Bethel police of Anjiras's disappearance and had given them a picture of Anjiras in August 1976.

The Bethel police reported on August 13, 1976, before being advised of Anjira's disappearance. During a large party, the Bethel police had observed a female matching Anjira's descriptions lying on the Charter Oaks Motorcycle's front lawn clubhouse.

The Bethel police did not identify the female. The Bethel police advised the Norwalk police that members of the Charter Oaks Motorcycle club were known to hang out at the South End Pub located in Danbury, Connecticut.

The bartender at the pub reported he knew Anjiras but did not know where she lived.

The Norwalk police had conducted surveillance of the pub and motorcycle clubhouse in Bethel, but Anjiras was not found; at the time, several motorcycle club members had been associated with multiple gang rapes and murders.

In November of 1975, two Charter Oaks Motorcycle club members had shot and killed three Norwalk residents in a Darien bar (Darien, Connecticut) after an argument.

On August 27, 1976, it was reported that Anjiras was involved in a fight with another female at the "Top of the Hill" tavern in Danbury, Connecticut.

The Bethel police eventually identified the female by using a Bethel school yearbook. When questioned by police, the female said she did not know Anjiras.

At the time of the investigation, the Bethel police had found a young female lying on the ground in front of the Charter Oak Motorcycle club. The seventeen-year-old female was not Anjiras.

The Anjiras case remains open.

Dawn Peterson

Missing: March 26, 1976

North Windham, Connecticut

DOB: October 13, 1962

On March 26, 1976, 13-year-old Dawn Peterson was found murdered a block away from her home in North Windham.

Peterson's body was found in an abandoned cellar in North Windham, Connecticut; Peterson had been bludgeoned to death with a rock.

A juvenile suspect, later identified as Andrew Carr, a neighbor, was charged with the crime. At the time of Peterson's death, Carr was a 15-year-old juvenile. After being arrested, the suspect was released on bail because of his age.

A hearing was held to determine if Carr should be tried in the Connecticut Court of Juvenile Matters or Superior Court and tried as an adult. On May 21, 1976, the suspect turned 16, and the case was transferred to the Superior Court for disposition.

On July 07, 1976, Carr appeared in Superior Court and was advised of his rights; Carr was released to his father's custody.

The court ordered the case file sealed, and the case jacket was entitled "State vs. Anonymous."

On September 02, 1976, the grand jury returned a bill of indictment charging Carr with the murder of Dawn Peterson.

The court ordered unsealed files but permitted the defendant to appeal the decision.

The court concluded that; (1) the defendant has no statutory to the file remain sealed; (2) on July 07, 1976, the court motion, sealing the record was based on the premise that Carr was entitled to the protection of confidentiality as a juvenile until such time the indictment was returned against him as an adult; (3) Carr was no longer allowed the protection of privacy.

The defense claimed: (a) a juvenile charged with a crime is entitled from stigmatizing publicity; (b) the policy of the state is to rehabilitate, not punish juvenile offenders; (c) the defendant was entitled to the same protection of confidentiality in the Superior Court that he was afforded in the Court of Juvenile Matters; the Superior Courts failure to reverse the motion to unseal the files violated Carr's presumption of innocence and right to privacy guaranteed by the United States constitution.

Andrew Carr was eventually acquitted of the crime.

Dawn Peterson's homicide is still considered unsolved.

Geraldine Lisbon

Missing: March 10, 1977

East Hartford, Connecticut

DOB: 1945

Lisbon is a 32-year-old white female, 5-05" tall, 120 Pounds, with brown hair, brown eyes, and a scar on her nose.

Lisbon was employed by an advertising agency in Hartford, Connecticut, and resided at 1270 Silver Lane in East Hartford, Connecticut.

Lisbon reported that her estranged husband, Arthur Lisbon (aka Tony Collins), had beaten her and burglarized her apartment the night before her disappearance.

Her estranged husband reported being released from a mental hospital a day before his wife's disappearance.

He said he had been drinking heavily during his wife's disappearance and heard "Cat like voices" that told him to abduct his wife so he could reconcile with her.

It was reported on March 07, 1977, at approximately 7:30 am, witnesses, including Geraldine's brother Robert, observed Geraldine's estranged husband kick down the front of Geraldine's residence and drag her out of the house to a parking lot across the street from her apartment and forced her into his car.

So why hadn't Geraldine's brother done anything to stop the assault?

Her estranged husband told authorities he had put Geraldine on a bus to Boston, Massachusetts, to visit her old college classmates. However, Geraldine never finishes high school.

Like the April Grisanti (1985) case, Geraldine's estranged husband, Arthur Lisbon, was only charged with his wife's abduction and other unrelated narcotics offenses.

Samuel Byrd

Missing: June 01, 1977

Hamden, Connecticut

DOB: July 14, 1958

Byrd is a 18-year-old African American male 5-09" tall, 170 pounds, with black hair and brown eyes.

Byrd was last seen after he graduated from Hamden High School.

Byrd was last seen in a limousine at the Tweed New Haven Regional Airport (New Haven, Connecticut).

Authorities believe that Byrd left on his own accord.

It is uncertain if Byrd had boarded an aircraft.

Byrd's classmates believe he was murdered because Byrd was close to his family, and he would have stayed in contact with them.

Byrd was reported missing in 2014 by family members, thirty-seven years after his disappearance.

Patricia Ellen Luce (aka Pattie)

Missing: July 18, 1978 (Homicide)

Vernon, Connecticut

DOB: 1960

Luce is a 18-year-old female who disappeared on July 18, 1978, at 20:30 hours after being dropped off by her brother at a seven-eleven convenience store on Route #83 in the Rockville section of Vernon, Connecticut.

Police believe that before Luce's disappearance, she may have been walking on Dart Hill Road in the direction of her home on Skinner Road.

Luce's skeletal remains were found along an abandoned gravel bank by two people walking in an isolated wooded area in Marlborough, Connecticut, on March 13, 1979.

The gravel bank is located on Hodge Road, approximately fifteen miles from where Luce was last seen.

During the investigation, Luce's then-boyfriend was considered a person of interest. Other rumors suggest Luce had been dating a teacher. One resident said there were apparent similarities between the Luce and Susan LaRosa homicides, reinforcing the local belief that all the cases were linked.

The state medical examiner Dr. Elliot Gross reported the case was considered a homicide; Luce had sustained a blunt-force trauma injury to her head.

(Rockville Cheerleaders Lisa Joy White and Patricia Luce)

Many residents believe there is a connection between the disappearances of the seven young females in the Vernon area over the past decade, while Vernon police Chief Herman Fritz said, "He doesn't believe there is a link in the cases."

"Both of the bodies had almost identical head injuries and were left unburied in the woods," Jerry Kelly, whose stepdaughter Lisa Joy White disappeared on November 01, 1974.

I believe Kelly was right; the number of disappearances in the Vernon area indicated a geographic predator. I don't think Chief Fritz had a dam clue. Kelly said, "I think it's someone who lives in the area that was doing it, and I think it will happen again to someone else unless the police catch him" (Hartford Courant, March 16, 1979).

Although there were similarities in the Susan LaRosa and Patricia Luce cases, the authorities reported they did not have any solid leads or links. The witness was described as a 25-year-old white male with curly hair and a mustache. It is believed he owned the dark-colored vehicle.

INFORMATION WANTED

THE CONNECTICUT STATE POLICE DEPARTMENT AND THE VERNON POLICE DEPARTMENT

We are investigating the disappearance of Patricia Luce, age 18, a white female, 5'7" tall, 135 lbs., brown hair and hazel eyes. Miss Luce was last seen on July 18, 1975, at about 9:00PM, walking toward her home in Vernon, Connecticut.

We are seeking to identify a WHITE MALE, about 25 years old, who may have important information in this case. The artist drawing above is believed to be a good likeness of the white male we seek. He is believed to be the owner and/or operator of a black or dark colored Thunderbird vehicle, similar to that pictured above.

It is requested that this matter be brought to the attention of all patrolmen and detectives and that patrolmen be alerted to watch for and report male subjects with similar facial characteristics and vehicles.

Any person having information contact the Connecticut State Police Department, toll free at 1-800-842-0200, or the Vernon Police Department at 1-203-872-9126.

CONNECTICUT STATE POLICE DEPARTMENT   Case: Y-75-0118-C
Detective Division
294 Colony Street
Meriden, CT 06450

Attn: Trooper James Johnston
       Tel. 566-7896

(CSP Suspect and Vehicle in Patricia Luce's Case)

Authorities told the author they eventually identified the individual in the sketch as an individual working in the area. Still, they did not believe he had any involvement in the case.

Another factor to consider is the change in the suspect(s) Modus of Operandi. The victim's bodies from 1968 to 1974 were hidden, and their bodies were never found. The victims' bodies from 1975-to 1978 were older and dumped, not hidden.

The change in the Modus of Operandi is significant; it could suggest the suspect(s) might have been sending a message to authorities, "Catch me if you can." The victim's age ranges from 1975-to 1978 increased from younger children to teenagers or young adult females.

The change in the suspect's Modus of Operandi indicates two different psychological profiles; the two patterns are divided by the victim's age. Profile (A) suggests the suspect prefers younger, more vulnerable children easily persuaded or physically over-powered; the suspect buries the bodies to hide them. The suspect may bury the body to conceal the crime and distance himself from evil. Profile (B) indicates the suspect prefers older females; the nature of the victim's injuries are identical. The suspect did not attempt to hide the bodies adequately; he wanted the bodies to be found for his notoriety; the pattern indicates the suspect believes he is more intelligent than the authorities and considers the police not to be a threat.

In all the cases, the victims' bodies were found a distance from where they were last seen. This indicates the victims either voluntarily or had been forced into a vehicle. The victims were picked up along the main road. The later victims all sustained a blunt force trauma injury to the head. The bodies were all discovered in remote areas, and there was no attempt to hide the bodies. The victims were all white females, ages 15-20, with similar physical characteristics. The roadside disappearances began after Susan LaRosa's homicide (1973).

Modus of Operandi and the Numbers

In 1975 the victim's race, age, gender, and manner of death changed.

Bodies Hidden:

July 24, 1968	Debra Spickler, (13)	
Mar. 01, 1971	Irene LaRosa, (17)	**Younger Females**
July 23, 1973	Janice Pockett, (7)	
Nov. 01, 1974	Lisa Joy White, (13)	

Change in Modus of Operandi

Bodies not Hidden:

June 22, 1975	Susan LaRosa, (20)	
July 21, 1975	Stephanie Olisky (15)	
July 18, 1978	Patricia Luce, (18)	**Older Females**
Aug. 27, 1978	Janette Reynolds, (17)	

The Numerological Aspect

The dates and months of the homicides and disappearances indicate a numeric consistency, the month of "July" and the numbers 21, 22, 23, and 24 frequently appear.

Special Force To Probe Vernon Disappearances

By MANIRA WILSON

VERNON — A special task force is being formed to investigate a possible connection between the apparent murder of 18-year-old Patricia Luce and the cases of four other area females who have disappeared in the last 10 years, state police said Thursday.

The skeletal remains of Miss Luce, who was reported missing July 18, were found in an isolated wooded area in Marlborough Tuesday. She was the fifth area female to disappear, and the second later found dead, since 1969.

Local residents fearing for the safety of their young girls last summer sought Gov. Grasso's help to force police to conduct more extensive searches around Vernon for Miss Luce. Those fears and cries for a more thorough investigation into all five cases were renewed Thursday.

The state's chief medical examiner, Dr. Elliot M. Gross, said Wednesday that Miss Luce's death is being considered a homicide. The body received head injuries, but an autopsy hadn't been completed by Thursday, a spokesman for Gross said.

Donald J. Long, state public safety commissioner, Thursday directed the police Major Crime Squad to form the special task force to review all the cases again to determine if there is a connection, a police spokesman said.

"The possibility of a connection had occurred to local and state police right along, but to date there has been no direct evidence" linking the cases, the spokesman said.

Vernon Police Chief Herman A. Fritz Jr. also said that local authorities still "don't see a connection at this point."

One resident said, however, that the apparent similarities between Miss Luce's death and that of 20-year-old Susan LaRosa, who disappeared in June 1975, have reinforced local belief that all the cases are linked.

The skeletal remains of Mrs. LaRosa were found May 18 by construction workers in a wooded area south of I-86. Her death has been termed a homicide, probably by a gunshot to the head.

"Both bodies had almost identical head injuries and both were left in the woods unburied," said Jerry Kelly, whose stepdaughter, Lisa White, disappeared in November 1977.

Police haven't been able to trace Lisa, 13, or the two other missing females, Deborah Speckler, who disap-

PATRICIA LUCE

peared from Henry Park in 1969 and Janice Pockett, 7, who last was seen near her Tolland home in July 1973.

"I think someone who lives in the area is doing it and I think it will happen again to someone else unless they (police) catch him," Kelly said.

Miss Luce last was seen about 9 p.m. near the Rt. 83

7-Eleven store where she had been dropped off by her younger brother about 8:30 p.m. The abandoned gravel bank where her body was found by two persons walking Tuesday afternoon is about 15 miles from where she last was seen.

Police have said they don't have any suspects in either the Luce or LaRosa case. Police are seeking a man as a potential witness in the Luce case. He has been described as about 25 years old with curly hair and a beard. He was believed to own or drive a black or dark-colored car.

Tolland county State's Attorney Donald B. Caldwell said he will ask Gov. Grasso to post a $20,000 reward for information in the Luce case. A $20,000 reward already has been posted in the LaRosa case.

Miss Luce's family and friends also already have raised about $5,000 in reward money.

(Patricia E. Luce Newspaper Article)

88

Children, Missing, Dead, Leave Puzzled Anguish

By HOWARD SHERMAN

Judith Kelly and Eleanor Lace used to sit in the stands at the Legion football field in Vernon to watch their daughters shake their way through cheerleading routines.

They didn't know each other very well but shared the small-talk of proud mothers.

Nine years later they are close friends and share the pain of losing their young girls.

Eighteen-year-old Patricia Lace was found murdered March 13 in a heavily wooded section near Hodge Road in Marlborough. She disappeared from the Vernon area July 18, last seen alive near a 7-Eleven store on Rt. 83, not far from her Skinner Road home.

Thirteen-year-old Lisa White, Mrs. Kelly's daughter from her first marriage, has not been found since she vanished Nov. 1, 1974 on her way back to her Regan Road home from a friend's house.

The two mothers try comforting each other with conversation over cups of coffee.

The two women lost contact for several years, until Mrs. Kelly telephoned Mrs. Lace when Patricia disap-

peared and asked if there was anything she could do.

"It's an awful way to bring people together, but now we're very close," said Mrs. Kelly.

While close to each other, they're still very far from finding out how their daughters disappeared.

The Lace and White girls are two of five Vernon area females who have disappeared during the last 10 years.

State police established a task force March 15 respecting investigations of all the cases, but no leads have been found. The three other cases are:

Seven-year-old Janice Pockett was last seen at her

Tolland home July 1973. She has never been found.

Twenty-year-old Susan LaRosa was found dead in May in a wooded section of Vernon south of I-86. No arrests have been made.

Fourteen-year-old Deborah Speckler vanished from Vernon's Henry Park in 1969 and has not been found.

Police across the country search for an estimated 22,000 missing persons on any given day, according to the National Crime Informa-

tion Center in Washington, D.C.

In 1978 Connecticut state police received 4,244 reports of missing persons.

"The amount of kids missing throughout the country is staggering," said state police spokesman Trooper John L. McLeod. Most of the persons reported missing are found or return home within hours, he said.

For the first few months after her daughter was gone, Mrs. Kelly couldn't accept her loss.

She crawled through abandoned buildings with her husband Gerald looking for clues. They sought help from a psychic, stopped passing cars and chased look-a-likes

through the woods hoping to find their daughter.

"You run into someone that looks like her and Christ, your heart stops. It brings everything back," said Mrs. Kelly sitting at her kitchen table.

But memories are the only things she found sloshing through swamps and walking along highways.

Sometimes she dreams about her daughter. "She's talking to me. She's saying, Mom I'll be back home in just a couple of more days," said the tall, dark-haired woman.

Mrs. Kelly sat cradling a

See They, Page 8

Decades after the disappearances and homicides, the authorities still could not identify a suspect(s) or establish a link to the cases. The author has a different opinion regarding the cases; it is said that with time, suspects and witnesses die or move. Still, time also provides us with more information and a broader landscape and timeline of the events. As previously mentioned, the disappearance of Irene LaRosa went unnoticed by authorities until 2016. The disappearance of Irene LaRosa (1971) and Susan LaRosa (1975) indicated a family as a suspect; however, the authorities did not recognize it at the time.

It was previously reported that three of the persons of interest in the LaRosa cases were acquaintances of the other victims. Unfortunately, the two prominent people of interest in these cases are deceased, and the third is outstanding.

I sent a copy of Berry P.'s statement to the state trooper investigating the case, he retired several months later, and the cases remain open. Although the two people of interest are deceased, it does not mean the investigations into the cases should end.

Their Lost Children Leave Anguish

Continued from Page 1

thick scrapbook in her arms which was filled with newspaper accounts of many missing children.

"I keep all the clippings about the skeletons, sex perverts, anything until I can ask the police about it," she said.

On the wall above her hung a collage of family photos. "The day she gave me that picture was the day she disappeared," said Mrs. Kelly pointing to her daughter's picture.

"I don't think I'll find her alive," but to find her at all would be enough.

Locating her daughter has made things somewhat easier for Mrs. Luce. "I wondered whether finding her was what I wanted," said the soft-spoken woman. She sat on the edge of a couch in a living room filled with condolence cards and funeral flowers.

"If she was found dead, I thought I would have no hope left. But now I feel more at peace."

Losing a family member strained both the Luce and Kelly families. "We tried to live as normal as possible, but it hurts inside," said Mrs. Luce. For a while, her daughter's disappearance made it difficult for Mrs. Kelly to deal with her two other children.

"It's not normal to have your child die before you do," Mrs. Kelly said. "You become overprotective with your other children and feel guilt about the missing child."

"My daughter walks alone only to the bus," said Mrs. Luce who has five boys and a 12-year-old daughter Marcia. All other times she's told to travel with her friends.

"I want to know where she is all the time," said Mrs. Luce. There are no guarantees that if it happened once it wouldn't happen again, she said.

To try to protect other children, Mrs. Luce and Mrs. Kelly are joining with area mothers to set up a self-defense course.

And the parents of the missing children keep searching.

James Conway, a private detective and Mrs. Kelly's friend, has spent endless

hours on his own "trudging down back paths and through woods," looking unsuccessfully for her daughter.

Unlike a murder, "there's no set formula" to solving a missing person case, said Conway. "It's a very painstaking quest."

Conway uncovered evidence which helped clear Peter A. Reilly of the charge he killed his mother Barbara Gibbons.

But all his work on the Lisa White case has produced nothing but dead ends.

State police share Conway's frustration. "You toss and turn and wake up (at night) wondering" if every clue has been followed, said retired state police Sgt. Richard Chapman.

Chapman has worked on many missing person cases and in retirement vividly recalls the hours he spent in jeeps, boats and on foot trying to find Connie Smith.

The 10-year-old granddaughter of former Wyoming Gov. Nels H. Smith has been missing for almost 27 years and is one of the department's oldest unsolved

missing person cases.

She was spending the summer at Camp Sloan in Salisbury while her mother Helen J. Smith visited her parents in Greenwich.

The young girl wandered from her cabin at 9 a.m. on the morning of July 16, 1952, and was seen asking directions to Lakeville, about a half mile away, but has never been found.

"We just about turned the place upside down" looking for her, said Chapman, who was the first investigator to arrive at the scene.

Yet American society is so mobile, a child could disappear from "Torrington and four days later wind up in California," said McLeod.

Police use computers, radios, helicopters and other equipment to track their missing persons. They depend on witnesses and research information as doubtful as a face in the photograph of a football crowd.

"There are so many possibilities it boggles the mind,"

said Trooper Andrew Rebmann.

Rebmann has been training state police search dogs for several years and has tracked several hundred missing persons. Even if the child is found, the policeman's task can still be difficult, he said.

Police have no power to bring back a person over the state's legal age of 18. "You check all the local hangouts," hoping to direct parents to their child," but there's not much more you can do," said Rebmann.

Deborah B. Leighton, director of a status offenders program for the state Department of Children and Youth Services, said many young people leave their homes because of family arguments. In a vulnerable emotional state, the instant affection and attention a pimp can provide may lure a young female into prostitution, she said.

Miss Leighton works with young runaways, mostly fe-

males 16 and under, who are considered juvenile offenders.

The 16-year-olds can be broken down into three groups said Miss Leighton: those running from a difficult home life, those running from what they consider the boredom at school or home and those leaving to gain attention — positive or negative.

Lisa White and Patricia Luce weren't runaways, said their mothers. They were shy girls who came from loving homes.

So now the mothers are looking for answers to their daughters' plights. In a soft, emotional voice, Mrs. Luce tells how she's contacted noted New Jersey psychic Dorothy Allison to help find their daughter's killers.

"I've got to know where she is," said Mrs. Kelly, fighting to hold back tears. "I'm her mother and I've got to know where she is."

But both women know it's not easy finding the answers.

JUDITH KELLY
"I don't think I'll find her alive."

ELEANOR LUCE
"Now I feel more at peace."

(Judy Kelly and Eleanor Luce)

Still No Trace

Over the years, the relationship between family members of the victims and the law enforcement agencies investigating the cases has become strained. The lack of suspects, links, and follow-ups has drawn harsh criticism from family members and the public.

Disappearance Probe Criticized

VERNON — The stepfather of a 13-year-old girl who disappeared about six months earlier than Susan LaRosa said the police are underplaying the relationship between those two disappearances and others over the last few years.

"He's entitled to his opinion," said Vernon Police Chief Herman A. Fritz Jr. "Anytime a female body shows up within half the state, the police department has in mind (other) missing persons," he said.

Police Tuesday flew a helicopter over the isolated wooded area where the skeleton of Susan LaRosa was found on Thursday. Photographs of the area were taken from the air. Fritz said helicopter and ground searches covered the area south of I-86 and east of Banforth Road where Mrs. LaRosa's remains were found.

Kelley, however, claimed police aren't fully investigating the relationship between several disappear-ances of young females in the area, including that of his stepdaughter, Lisa White, who was last seen in Rockville in November 1974.

Lisa disappeared from her home on Prospect Street, only a block away from the Ward Street tene-ment where Mrs. LaRosa was living at the time of her disappearance.

Police have said they have no rea-son to suspect foul play in the La-Rosa case, but Kelly maintains that Mrs. LaRosa and his stepdaughter were murdered.

Police are awaiting a report from the state medical examiner on the cause of Mrs. LaRosa's death. "If the medical examiner says murder, and that's an if, I would have no prime suspect," Fritz said. Fritz wouldn't comment on reports that the LaRosa woman's skull was nicked or dented, conditions that might suggest a bullet wound or blow to the head.

"All we want to do is bury Lisa,"

Kelly said. The family has no hope of finding her alive or finding her killer, he said. But "People should be scared" because then "maybe they'll watch their kids more care-fully this summer."

He said he thinks another disap-pearance case, that of 9-year-old Janice Pockett, last seen near her Tolland home in July 1973, also is related.

"Walk about five miles down the road from the spot where Susan La-Rosa's body was found and you'll come to Janice Pockett's house," Kelly said.

Fritz said state and local police are cooperating on the investigation, but Kelly said friction between the two departments has hampered it.

"It seems like nobody gives a damn," Kelly said.

He vowed to conduct his own search of the area if police efforts continue to turn up no clues.

(Families Criticize Investigation into Disappearances)

The author noted several stumbling blocks in the cases; the authorities had divided the case into two primary categories, disappearances, and homicides, reducing the statistical overview of the crimes. All the cases began as abductions leading to homicide.

The victims were all young white females divided into two age classifications; this indicates the suspect(s) had a specific age range for selecting their victims.

Between 1968 and 1974, the victims were younger white females, and their bodies were hidden. Between 1975 and 1978, the victims were teenagers and adults; there was no attempt to hide the bodies.

1968	Debra Spickler	
1971	Irene LaRosa	**(Bodies Hidden)**
1973	Janice Pockett	
1974	Lisa Joy White	

(Division Line Between Disappearances and Homicides)

1975	Susan LaRosa	
1975	Stephanie Olisky	**(Bodies not Hidden)**
1978	Patricia Luce	
1978	Janette Reynold	

Barbra Jean Monaco

Missing: August 23, 1978

Derby, Connecticut

DOB: August 19, 1960

Monaco is an 18-white female, 5-04" tall, 110 pounds, with brown hair and brown eyes. Monaco had suffered a hairline fracture to her left arm at the time of her disappearance; Monaco was blind in one eye.

Monaco was last seen wearing a long-sleeve yellow shirt, blue jeans, and brown belted clogs.

On August 20, 1978, Monaco and her older sister took a trip to Virginia Beach the day after Monaco's 18th birthday.

They had registered at the Aloha Motel located on 15th Street.

Later that night, Monaco and her older sister went to the Country Comfort bar. While at the bar, an unidentified male patron began making passes at Monaco. The man told Monaco he owned a yacht.

On August 23, 1973, at approximately 01:00 hours, Monaco left her sister at the bar and began walking on Pacific Avenue toward Peabody's bar. She planned a date with one of the bartenders.

Witnesses reported seeing Monaco walking on Pacific Avenue; one witness observed Monaco get into a vehicle occupied by four or five males. Monaco was never seen again.

Eight months after posting a $10,000 reward for information leading to Monaco's disappearance, a man only identified as "Condor" claimed to know about Monaco's rape and murder.

The man stated Monaco was forced into a vehicle as she walked on Pacific Avenue. The suspects then raped and murdered her at a lakeside cottage near Oceana, Virginia, and her body was dumped into the lake.

Authorities searched the lake and found a cinder block with a rope attached to it, but Monaco's body was never found.

The informant ceased his cooperation in the case when Andre Evans, the Commonwealth's Attorney, refused to offer him immunity from prosecution.

A person of interest, identified as James L. Moore Jr., made a statement to the police. The information included details (description of her shoes) of the crime, which could have only been known by someone involved in the abduction and murder.

Moore agreed to take a polygraph to authentic his story, but hours before taking the polygraph test Moore (1954-2001) committed suicide (carbon monoxide poisoning) outside his Laskin Road apartment. His body was found the following day.

Janette Reynolds (aka Jan)

August 27, 1978

Middletown, Connecticut

DOB: 1960

On August 27, 1978, 17-year-old Janette Reynolds vanished while hitchhiking from Middletown, Connecticut, to her home in Griswold, Connecticut.

Reynolds was last seen near Route #2 and Route #11 near the Four Corners section of Colchester, Connecticut. She was allegedly observed getting into a blue International Scout with a white top. The vehicle was last seen traveling east on Route #16.

On March 25, 1979, Reynolds's body was found under the Gold Star Memorial Bridge in Groton, Connecticut.

Her murder is still unsolved.

Joseph J. Kasak

Missing: May 09, 1980

Newington, Connecticut

DOB: February 21, 1937

Kasak is a 43-year-old white male, 5-07" tall, 185 pounds, with black hair and brown eyes.

Kasak was last seen on May 09, 1980, at his residence in Newington, Connecticut.

At approximately 5:30 am, Kasak's vehicle was involved in a single-vehicle accident on Route 9 in Keene, New Hampshire.

An extensive search was conducted in the vicinity of the accident; however, Kasak was never found; a well-being check of Kasak's residence in Connecticut was done and provided no additional information.

It has not been determined who was operating the vehicle at the time of the accident.

Martin Alan Miller

Missing: May 1980

West Hartford, Connecticut

DOB: 1962

Miller is a 18-year-old white male, 5-10" tall, 165 pounds, with brown hair and hazel eyes. Miller has a small appendectomy scar on his abdomen.

Miller was last seen in May of 1980 in West Hartford, Connecticut. Miller had given his employer (McDonald's) his two-week notice and told his friends he was going to California.

Miller closed his bank accounts and rented an Avis rental car.

Miller had left his two vehicles at home and had given his expensive bicycle to a friend. Miller's rental car was located ten days later in Huntsville, Alabama.

Miller's disappearance wasn't reported until 1999, nineteen years after his disappearance. Miller's parents said that although Martin was brilliant, he had a psychological disorder.

It is believed Miller might have had suicidal tendencies at the time of his disappearance.

Keith A. LaLima

Missing: May 07, 1981

Norwich, Connecticut

DOB: May 27, 1960

Laima is a 20-year-old white male 6-01" tall, 175 pounds, with brown hair and hazel eyes.

LaLima was last seen wearing a blue plaid shirt, blue dungarees, brown shoes, a blue baseball cap, and a silver necklace or medallion. LaLima was seen at approximately 1:00 am outside the Old Village Green Café near West Main Street and Maple Street in Norwich, Connecticut.

Before LaLima's disappearance, witnesses observed LaLima arguing with a man outside the bar. LaLima was last seen walking in the direction of his mother's (Katherine Helm) apartment on Oakwood Knoll, where he lived with his girlfriend, Jacky Pavlik, and their young son.

His mother's apartment is located approximately two miles away from the bar. When LaLima failed to return home or go to work the following day, his mother reported him missing.

The Norwich police believe LaLima was a victim of a violent crime and that his body was hidden somewhere in Norwich.

The search included dredging several local ponds and the Yantic River after a person had reported to police that LaLima's body had been thrown into the river.

The Norwich police have interviewed several persons of interest in the LaLima case, but no arrests have been made.

Jovonna Stacey Crawford

Missing: June 05, 1981

Bridgeport, Connecticut

DOB: August 29, 1979

Crawford is a 21-year-old African American female, 2-01" tall, 30 pounds, with black hair and brown eyes. Crawford was last seen wearing a blue and white jumpsuit.

At the time of her disappearance, Jovonna Crawford was being watched at her home by her mother's then-boyfriend Ronald Garrett. Crawford resided in Building 8, apartment 208, in Bridgeport, Connecticut's PT Barnum housing project.

On the date of the disappearance, Crawford's mother, Mary Corbin, was running late for work and had asked Garrett to watch Jovonna for a short time. Crawford was then to be brought to her maternal great-grandmother's (Mary Morales) apartment by Garrett.

When Corbin returned home from work, Garrett told Corbin that at 10:30 am, a ten or 11-year-old African American boy with small braids came to the door and told Garrett he was there to take Jovonna to her grandmother's apartment.

Garrett reported to the police that he gave Jovonna to the young boy; the young boy was never identified if he did exist.

100

Jovonna's grandmother Mary Morales said she never sent anyone to the apartment to pick the baby up.

Garrett was arrested for Jovonna's disappearance and was sentenced to ten months in prison for the girl's disappearance. Garrett now resides in Georgia and is not cooperating with the police.

Jovonna's mother said she believed Garrett had something to do with the disappearance because Garrett never showed any signs of remorse.

Edward Sprenkler Dubbs

Missing: June 09, 1981

Newtown, Connecticut

DOB: January 19, 1937

Dubbs is a 44-year-old white male 5-10" tall, 150 pounds, with curly sandy blonde hair, blue eyes, and metal-rimmed prescription aviator-style glasses.

Dubbs was last seen wearing a beige silk business suit and a gold digital "Timex" wristwatch.

Dubbs was seen leaving his place of employment at the Hayes-Williams Corporation, a public relations company located at 261 Madison Avenue in Manhattan, New York, Dubbs was a top-level executive at the time of his disappearance.

Dubbs would commute from his home in Connecticut to work by train to Grand Central Station in New York. Dubbs would return home and get off at the Redding or Bethel train station in Connecticut.

While on the train, Dubbs frequented the train's bar, which served alcoholic beverages. Dubbs left his office at approximately 5:05 pm to catch the train home on the day of his disappearance.

When Dubbs failed to show up to work the following day (Wednesday), his employer contacted the Newtown Police and requested the police conduct a well-being check at Dubbs' residence.

When police arrived at Dubbs's residence on Taunton Lane in Newtown, Connecticut, the police reported no vehicles or people at his home.

Police reported that Dubbs's residence showed no evidence that he had returned home on the day of his disappearance.

Dubbs's live-in boyfriend reported dropping Dubbs off at the Bethel train station that morning at approximately 6:00 am, and he returned to pick him up later that evening.

Dubbs's boyfriend reported that Dubbs was not there when he got to the Bethel train station that evening, so he drove to the Redding train station, but he could not locate Dubbs.

The boyfriend reported that it was not uncommon for Dubbs to stay in New York overnight.

At the time of the disappearance, Dubbs tried to end his relationship with his boyfriend, who was twenty-one years younger. Dubbs's boyfriend still resides in Northeastern Connecticut.

At the time of the disappearance, Dubbs owned a blue 1978 Mercury-Zephyr bearing Connecticut license plate PB-3985.

Charles Lewis Lassell, Jr.

Missing: October 27, 1981

Mystic, Connecticut

DOB: January 27, 1962

Lassell is a 19-year-old white male, 6-02" tall, 190 pounds, with brown hair, blue eyes, and a scar on the outside corner of his right eye.

At approximately 7:30 am, his father dropped off Lassell at the bus stop at Jerry Browne Road and Coogan Boulevard in Old Mystic, Connecticut.

Lassell would wait for the bus to take him to the local college. It was reported that Lassell never boarded the bus and was never seen again.

Julianne Miller (aka Julianne Miller)

Missing: September 22, 1982

Old Saybrook, Connecticut

DOB: July 18, 1955

Miller is a 32-year-old white female, 5-06" tall, 110 pounds, with blonde hair and blue eyes.

At the time of Miller's disappearance, Miller had been dating her live-in boyfriend, James Clayton.

Miller and Clayton resided in a cottage on Clinton Avenue, located in Old Saybrook, Connecticut. Miller's father had initially owned the cottage but later transferred the ownership over to his daughter (Julianne Miller).

During their dating relationship, Miller had transferred half of the property (cottage) ownership over to her live-in boyfriend. On September 20, 1982, Miller requested that Clayton sign his half of the property back to her.

On September 21, 1982, at approximately 11 pm, a tenant residing with Miller and Clayton reported that he last saw Miller and Clayton in the living room watching television.

The tenant reported it appeared Miller and Clayton were involved in an argument. This was the last time Miller was seen.

105

A witness reported that after Miller disappeared, Clayton had rearranged the furniture in the cottage, and the witness observed some of the couch cushions missing. Clayton told the witness he had brought the cushions to the dry cleaners.

Miller's live-in boyfriend never reported her missing.

Clayton reported to police that he last saw Miller on September 22, 1982, getting into a brown pick-up truck operated by an African American male.

Clayton was an African American male who owned a brown pick-up truck.

Authorities later found Miller's vehicle, dog, purse, and unsigned quick claim deed for the cottage's property.

Immediately after Miller's disappearance, her boyfriend told the two tenants living in the cottage to leave.

Authorities administrated a polygraph test to both tenants, which they both passed. Clayton refused to take a polygraph test.

Authorities discovered blood on the cushions and in the springs of the couch. However, DNA testing was not available in 1982.

The sofa cushions had been previously cleaned with bleach.

Miller's relatives reported that several pieces of her jewelry were found missing. Clayton's brother later discovered that the missing jewelry was hocked at a local pawnshop.

It is believed that Clayton murdered Miller in the cottage and buried her body on the property which borders the Cockaponset State Forest.

In 2002 Clayton, a Captain in the Army medical corps, was charged with attempted murder after fracturing a soldier's skull with a hammer during an attempted robbery.

Michael Fischer (aka Mike)

Missing: August 14, 1984

Bloomfield, Connecticut

DOB: 1965

Fischer is a 19-year-old white male, 5-06" tall, 160 pounds, with blonde hair and blue eyes.

Fischer was last seen by family members on August 14, 1984, at his mother's funeral in Bloomfield, Connecticut.

Family members received a postcard from Fischer in early September of 1987 postmarked from Florida.

Family members received a second postcard in late September of 1987; the letter was postmarked from Knoxville, Tennessee.

No other information is available.

Mary Edna Badaracco (aka Mary Poo)

Missing: August 19, 1984

Sherman, Connecticut

DOB: August 11, 1946

Badaracco is a 34-year-old white female, 5-07" tall, 145 pounds, with brown hair and brown eyes; she has a surgical scar on her abdomen, a scar on her right thumb, and psoriasis on her elbows and knees; she had front dentures and pierced ears.

Badaracco was a self-employed house cleaner at the time.

Her marriage to Dominic Badaracco was unstable at the time of her disappearance, and there were claims of infidelities and domestic violence. She was separated from her husband and was in the process of a divorce.

Dominic Badaracco claimed he last saw his wife on August 20, 1984, at their residence on Wakeman Hill Road, in Sherman, Connecticut.

Her husband claimed his wife had taken her belongings and left the house after receiving a telephone call. Her husband claimed he had given his wife $100,000 - $250,000 (He didn't remember how much money he gave her) as an informal settlement before leaving the house.

Badaracco's wedding ring and car keys were found on the kitchen counter. Her 1982 Chevrolet Cavalier was found at the end of the driveway with its front driver-side window smashed.

Her husband admitted smashing the car window, but the police failed to seize the vehicle for evidence. The car disappeared sometime later and has never been seen again. There are no records of the car being stolen, sold, or re-registered.

Dominic had filed for a divorce on the grounds of abandonment two days before his wife went missing.

Like the Susan LaRosa case, a woman and her daughter moved into the Badaracco residence less than a week after Mary Badaracco's disappearance.

Dominic reported he moved out of the house and was living with his sister at the time of his wife's disappearance, and he reported he was renting the home to the woman and her daughter; he later married the same woman.

It was rumored that Badarocco's son was a member of a motorcycle gang that had been responsible for the homicide.

April L Grisanti

Missing: February 01, 1985

Norwalk, Connecticut

DOB: May 01, 1964

Grisanti is a 20-year-old white female, 5-04" tall, 120 pounds, with brown hair, brown eyes, and pierced ears.

Grisanti was last seen wearing a black shirt, black rabbit-fur coat, blue jeans, white sneakers, a thin silver ring with a turquoise stone, silver earrings, and a gray/blue clutch purse with a zipper top.

Shortly after midnight, Grisanti left Anthony's Café, located at 174 Main Street in Norwalk, Connecticut.

Grisanti had walked across the street to use the telephone to call for a ride. Her boyfriend accompanied Grisanti, James "Purple" Aaron Jr. A witness observed Grisanti struggling with Aaron inside his blue Cadillac as it turned onto Main Street. A half-hour before Grisanti's disappearance, she had been assaulted by Aaron and called the police. During the assault, Grisanti sustained a bloody finger; however, she refused to press charges against Aaron.

Grisanti's vehicle was later found in the Norwalk River near Ann Street. A month later, Grisanti's wallet and driver's license were dumped along a road in Norwalk.

In 1981 Aaron's estranged wife, Mary Frattalone-Aaron, disappeared from their residence. A month later, her body was found in a wooded area behind a commuter parking lot along Route 123. The couple was in the process of filing for a divorce.

In 1981 Aaron had been charged with following a woman to the rear of Anthony's Café; he then pushed the female into a corner and punched her; as a result of the assault, the victim sustained a swollen eye. Aaron threatened the female that "He would kill her by tomorrow" if she said anything to the police.

Aaron was only charged with abducting and unlawful restraint in the Grisanti case. Aaron was convicted and served six years in prison; Aaron was released from prison in 1991.

Grisanti's mother, Lou Grisanti, filed a lawsuit against Aaron for injuries her daughter sustained during the abduction; the suit was settled in 1992 for $50,000.

Aaron was never charged for Mary Frattalone-Aaron or April Grisanti's homicide. Aaron died in 2016 and is still considered the prime person of interest in both homicides.

Rosa Maria Valentin (aka Rosita and Coco)

Missing: July 26, 1986

Hartford, Connecticut

DOB: 1970

Valentin is a 16-years old white female, 5-02" tall, 115 pounds, with black hair, brown eyes, with a mole on her right cheek.

Valentin was wearing blue jeans, a cotton shirt with numbers, a Battiston Cleaner dress, white shoes, a long strapped black pocketbook, and a silver chain necklace with a unicorn charm.

Valentin was last seen in Hartford, Connecticut, getting into a white Ford-Cobra operated by a 29-year-old acquaintance named Pedro Miranda; Miranda had a lengthy criminal history of violent crimes that started in 1977. Mayra Cruz (1987) and Carmen Lopez (1988) were abducted in Hartford, Connecticut, and later found strangled. Miranda claimed the witnesses who observed Rosa Valentin get into his car on July 26, 1986, were mistaken.

(Pedro Miranda)

(Mayra Cruz)   (Carmen Lopez)

In 2011 Miranda was convicted of abducting and murdering Carman Lopez Miranda received a life sentence without the possibility of parole.

In 2015 Miranda was charged with the murder of Mayra Cruz and sentenced to life without the possibility of parole.

Miranda was never charged with Valentin's murder.

The prosecutor dropped the charges against Miranda in Valentin's murder case, citing problems with the evidence.

Valentin is still considered a missing person.

Regina F. Brown

Missing: March 26, 1987

Newtown, Connecticut

DOB: December 04, 1951

Brown is a 36-year-old light-skinned African American female of Creole descent, 5-03" tall, 115 pounds, with black hair, brown eyes, with a cesarean section scar on her abdomen.

Brown wears her hair pulled back in a ponytail, and she is missing three of her teeth.

Brown was last seen wearing a white fleece sweater, white sweatpants with a tan stripe, tan snakeskin shoes, and a gold rope necklace with a diamond pendant.

At the time of her disappearance, Brown resided on Whippoorwill Hill Road in Newtown, Connecticut, and was employed by American Airlines.

Brown was last seen at LaGuardia Airport in New York while returning home from the airport. Brown called her best friend and told her, "If no one hears from her in four days, something happened to her." It was reported that Brown was afraid of her estranged husband, Willis Brown; Brown told her friend that her estranged husband said, "He would have done to me what he promised to do to me."

On March 27, 1987, neighbors contacted the police because Regina's dog had been barking.

Brown subsequently missed a lunch date with her best friend and failed to show up for two flight assignments at work. Brown's estranged husband was a senior pilot at American Airlines at her disappearance.

Brown's employer contacted her parents. Her parent got Regina's best friend and asked her to check their daughter's house.

On April 02, 1987, Brown's best friend arrived at the house and found her dog locked in the garage.

Brown's best friend noticed two bags of dog food in the garage; it was not the brand of dog food Brown typically bought.

Most of Regina's personal; property, airline identification, make-up bag, and a $1,000 check were found at the house.

Brown's best friend and Brown's estranged husband, Willis Brown, filed a missing person's report.

There were custodial issues between Regina and Willis at the time of the disappearance. Brown and her estranged husband were in the process of a divorce.

A court protective order was in place at the time of the disappearance banning Willis Brown from going to Regina's Newtown home. On March 26, 1987, the estranged husband said he brought dog food to the house before his dentist appointment in Newtown.

The estranged husband told police that he went back to his apartment in Queens after going to the house, and they (police) should look for Brown's car in Manhattan, New York. How would the husband know where to look for the vehicle?

On April 06, 1987, Brown's beige Honda-Accord hatchback was in front of an apartment building at 104th Street in Manhattan, New York; the keys were still in the ignition. The area is known for illegal drug sales.

Regina's mother died in Liberty, Texas, on August 01, 2006, at the age of 83.

Brown's estranged husband is considered a person of interest in the case but has never been charged.

Elizabeth Kovalik (aka Elizabeth Monks)

Missing: November 13, 1987

Milford, Connecticut

DOB: 1959

Kovalik is a 28-year-old white female, 5-05" tall, 144 pounds, with brown hair, brown eyes, and a birthmark on her inner right forearm.

Kovalik was last seen wearing a brown sweater and blue jeans. Kovalik resided on Burton Road in Milford, Connecticut, and was the mother of a three-year-old son.

Kovalik was employed at the Dictaphone Company located in Stratford, Connecticut. Before her disappearance, Kovalik had been absent from work on November 09 and November 11, 1987; Kovalik returned to work on November 13, 1987.

A coworker reported that she was acting strange when Kovalik returned to work.

On November 13, 1987, Kovalil was seen with two male acquaintances before leaving for McKenna's bar on Chapel Street in New Haven, Connecticut; this was the last time Kovalik was seen. One of the male acquaintances reported he dropped Kovalik off in front of her residence on Burton Road in Milford, Connecticut, on November 15, 1987.

Another version of the story was that Kovalik met two male acquaintances at a bar in New Haven on November 14, 1987. One of the acquaintances said he dropped her off on her street on November 15, 1987.

Family members became concerned when Kovalik failed to attend a Thanksgiving dinner; it was uncharacteristic for Kovalik to miss a family holiday.

Family members said it was common for Kovalik not to show up for a few days, but she would always keep in contact.

Kovalik's father reported her missing on November 22, 1987. Kovalik's father died in 2008 without knowing his daughter's fate.

It was reported that drugs were involved in the case, and Kovalik had met with foul play.

Doreen Jane Vincent

Missing: June 05, 1988

Wallingford, Connecticut

DOB: September 30, 1975

Vincent is a 12-year-old white female, 5-04" tall, 110 pounds, with brown hair, hazel eyes, a mole on her abdomen, and double-pierced ears.

Vincent was last seen at her father's residence on 316 Whirlwind Hill Road in Wallingford, Connecticut, between 8:00 and 9:00 pm. Before leaving home, Vincent was involved in an argument with her father, Mark, a contractor working in Milford, Connecticut.

Her father reported that Doreen took money and clothes and left the house through the front door. Doreen was never seen again. Her father stated he last saw his daughter in the kitchen before going into his workshop.

Her father's workshop was a barn behind the house, which was suspiciously torn down by the property owner James Farnam a short time after Doreen's disappearance.

On June 15, 1988, Sharon Vincent (deceased) said she had cooked dinner for her family, including the two younger children, and then left for a church service in West Haven. This fact was never confirmed.

Mark Vincent, age 55, said he returned home from his workshop at 9:00 pm and discovered his daughter was not in her bedroom.

Sharon said she arrived home from church at 9:30 pm and was advised by her husband that Doreen was missing and that he was going to Bridgeport, Connecticut, to look for her. It was never confirmed if Mark ever went to Bridgeport.

In a statement made by Doreen's stepmother, she said it would have been impossible for Doreen to have left through the front door because the door was deadbolted from the inside, and only she and her husband had the key.

Sharon stated the front door was locked when she left the house, and the door was locked when she returned home.

Mark's wife, Sharon, said her husband had a violent temper, and before Doreen's disappearance, he had pushed Doreen into a window causing the window to shatter.

After the disappearance, Mark went to visit his mother, Lorraine Vincent, but Mark failed to tell his mother that Doreen was missing.

Mark said he did not tell his mother about Doreen's disappearance because his mother was not part of Doreen's life.

Doreen's mother, Donna Lee, reported she attempted to call her ex-husband (Mark) on June 17, 1988, but no one answered the telephone. It was later learned that Mark had removed the phone from the wall.

Donna Lee and her sister Carol arrived at her ex-husband's house on June 18, 1988, to get Doreen. Until this point, Mark failed to tell Doreen's mother about their daughter's disappearance.

When Doreen's mother and her sister arrived at Mark's house to get Doreen, they found him pouring a cement patio in front of the house.

Interestingly enough, in 2018, thirty-one years after Doreen's disappearance, the owner of the home (James Farnam) where Doreen lived at the time of her disappearance reported that he was unaware that Doreen's father, Mark, had poured a cement patio in front of the house.

My first thought was, what was under the cement patio and how was the home unaware of the cement slab being poured?

When Doreen's mother had asked her ex-husband about her daughter's whereabouts, Mark said he had sent Doreen to stay at her maternal grandmother's house. "He insisted I sent her to my mother's house," Lee said; her ex-husband told her he did not want to report his daughter missing.

Mark previously said that Doreen hadn't been a part of her maternal grandmother's life, so why would he bring her there to stay? It has been documented that Doreen's father, Mark, was seen near Huntington State Park at the time of his daughter's disappearance. Mark denies the accusation; however, Mark was observed by a park ranger carrying a large object into a wooded area of the park. The park is located near Doreen's maternal grandmother's house.

After observing Mark exit his truck and carry the wrapped object into the woods, the park ranger recorded the truck's license plate and completed a written report of the incident. My question is, why hadn't the park ranger stopped Mark?

A year after Doreen's disappearance, the police searched Mark's mother's (Lorraine Vincent's) Marywood Road home. The same truck identified by the park ranger, Mark's truck, contained a young girl's shirt with bloodstains.

On July 30, 1989, the police searched the maternal grandmother's home and garage and found clothing and property belonging to Doreen. The clothes matched Doreen's dress at the time of the disappearance.

The search also recovered a revolver and ammunition hidden in a paper bag in the grandmother's garage. The gun and forty rounds of ammunition belonged to her father, a convicted felon prohibited from owning a firearm or ammunition.

Mark Vincent was arrested and charged with possessing a firearm and ammunition by a convicted felon and sentenced to two years in prison.

Later that year, Mark and his wife Sharon separated. Mark moved out of the Wallingford home without leaving a forwarding address.

Doreen's mother had gone to the Whirlwind residence to collect Doreen's belongings. When Doreen's mother asked Sharon, "What happened to Doreen's matching bedsheet?" Sharon said Doreen had messed the bedsheets up, so Mark threw them out.

In the park ranger report, he stated the large object he saw Mark carry into the woods was wrapped in a multicolored cloth similar to Doreen's missing bed sheet.

When Sharon moved out of the Whirlwind home, she took Doreen's belongings and refused to turn them over to the police.

Sharon reported buying a revolver for Mark at the Silver City Gun shop under her name because Mark was a convicted felon.

After separating from Mark, Sharon sold the revolver back to the gun shop. Sharon reported that when Mark found out she had sold the gun, he became enraged and made her buy the pistol back.

Why did Mark get so enraged when Sharon sold the revolver?

He was a convicted felon and couldn't own a gun, or had the gun been evidence of a crime? Throughout the police interview with Mark and Sharon, their statements concerning the disappearance were conflicting and deceptive.

During an interview with Jessica Fritz-Aguiar, the owner of the Whirlwind home James Farnam made several bolstered, conflicting, and deceptive statements.

Farnam had rented the Whirlwind house to Mark Vincent; Mark had previously done work on Farnam's Fountain Street property in New Haven, but Farnam denied knowing Mark Vincent.

Farnam had previously known Mark Vincent from Team Challenge, a drug rehabilitation facility in Connecticut.

Farnam then later said he could not remember Marks's name.

Farnam attempted to distance himself from Doreen, only referring to her as "The girl that was missing," however, in a later statement, he knew what type of clothes Doreen wore (apply: Beatle Juice comment).

Farnam said during the interview, "If I knew I was being recorded, I would have been more guarded," why would you be guarded?

Farnam then attempted to deflect his knowledge about the disappearance by saying, "They never found her?"

Farnam knew they hadn't found Doreen. Doreen's mother hired a private investigator, and the investigator had paid to have Farnam's septic tank in his yard drained to search for Doreen's body.

He knew the police were excavating areas on his property looking for Doreen's body, but he denied any knowledge of the events throughout the interview.

After the disappearance, Farnam had the barn (Mark's workshop) on the Whirlwind property torn down before the police searched it. I believe both Mark Vincent and James Farnam are people of interest in the case.

It's a known fact Mark was violent, and he had sexually abused females in the family, which brings up another disturbing point. Why was Mark taking pictures of his 13-year-old daughter in her underwear?

The Wallingford police denied seizing any pictures of Doreen in her underwear; however, during a later interview, Mark requested that the Wallingford police return the pictures to him.

Maybe he wanted the destroy the pictures.

I spoke with a reliable source who was told by a retired detective working on the case that they had seized pictures of Doreen in her underwear (Mark Vincent took the photos).

It was not mentioned that Mark had burnt Doreen's diary in the Whirlwind home driveway days after Doreen's disappearance.

In 2003 Mark believed he was dying from a chronic illness and told his lawyer he wanted to confess, but he wanted complete immunity.

Why would you need complete immunity if you didn't do anything?

Mark once said, "He would see Doreen in Heaven." This statement suggests that he already knew Doreen was dead.

(Refer: Fade Out - Sarah DiMeo, Joseph Aguiar, and Jessica Fritz-Aguiar)

Kenneth Scott Reed

Missing: March 24, 1989

Norwich, Connecticut

DOB: July 31, 1964

Reed is a 24-year-old white male 5-08" tall, 145 pounds, with blonde hair, brown eyes, and a mustache.

Reed was last seen wearing gray pants and white Niki Air Jordan sneakers with blue stripes.

On March 24, 1989, at approximately 3:26 pm, Reed left his job at the Bee Dairy in the Norwich Mall and drove to his parent's house on 20 Forest Street in Norwich, Connecticut. While enroute to his parent's house, Reed stopped to buy a cup of coffee. When Reed arrived at his parent's house to visit his disabled mother, he parked his vehicle in front of his parent's driveway.

Reed's unoccupied vehicle was found blocking the driveway by a neighbor. Reed's coffee was still inside the car, and there were no signs of a struggle. Ray Skidgel, a family friend, said, "When it came to his (Reed) coffee, he'll drink his coffee."

Reed's father reported that he saw his son's gray, four-door, Isuzu-Mark I parked in front of the house, but it was raining, so he did not go outside.

Skidgel said Kenneth would always lock his car doors and never block the driveway. In 1981 Reed started working as a dishwasher at the Bee Dairy, and in eight years, he had worked his way up to an assistant manager's position. Skidgel said, "Kenneth had become bored with the job and was occasionally depressed."

Reed worked at the Bee Dairy in Norwich, Connecticut, the same Bee Dairy frequented by Keith LiLima, who disappeared from Norwich, Connecticut, on May 07, 1981.

Weeks before Reed's disappearance, he had received two threatening telephone calls from an employee he had fired.

Reed had also been threatened by a man whose girlfriend he had been dating. The girlfriend had called Reed shortly before his disappearance.

Like most missing person cases, there were several reported sightings of Reed in the Norwich and Groton area after his disappearance, but none of the sightings were confirmed.

Marisela Pino: (aka Merisela Vazquez-Pino or Marisela Pino-Vazquez)

Missing: March 20, 1990

Waterbury, Connecticut

DOB: September 29, 1981

Pino is an 11-year-old Hispanic female 4-05" tall, 85 pounds, with brown hair, brown eyes, a scar on her left ankle, and a scar (burn) on her stomach and chest.

Pino was last seen wearing a black jacket, green and white shirt, green denim pants, white socks, and blue shoes.

Before her disappearance, Pino was last seen walking on Cherry Street in the vicinity of "Nash's Pizza" in Waterbury, Connecticut.

Mary Ann Kopacz

Missing: June 18, 1991

East Hartford, Connecticut

DOB: 1967

Kopacz is a 24-year-old white female, 5-01" tall, 105 pounds, with blonde hair and brown eyes.

Kopacz has a scar on her right hand, right arm, and nose. Kopacz was a known alcoholic.

On June 18, 1991, Kopacz was last seen in East Hartford, Connecticut. She disappeared under unknown circumstances.

Kopacz was not reported missing until October 03, 2001, ten years after her disappearance.

George Tsolakis (aka Georgie)

Missing: February 23, 1992

Marlborough, Connecticut

DOB: 1954

Tsolakis is a 38-year-old white male, 5-04", 200 pounds, with black hair, brown eyes, and a scar on the right side.

Tsolakis was last seen wearing dark gray nylon "Nike" pants, brown leather ankle boots, and a "Citizen" wristwatch with a silver/gold band.

Tsolakis was last seen at 11:30 pm on February 23, 1992, at the Greek American Sports Club on Maple Street in Marlborough, Connecticut.

Tsolakis had called his wife to say he was on his way home, but Tsolakis never arrived.

On March 20, 1992, a month after Tsolakis's disappearance, his red Fiat was covered in snow in the Foxwoods Casino's parking lot in Ledyard, Connecticut.

An employee at the casino reported on March 16, 1992, that he had issued Tsolakis a complimentary buffet ticket; however, the casino security camera footage had been erased, so the authorities could not identify the person in the video.

At the time of his disappearance, Tsolakis was in debt and unable to pay his creditors.

Some of Tsolaki's friends believe he was afraid of going to jail; some theorize Tsolakis had fled the country to avoid financial problems. Others said Tsolakis seemed depressed before his disappearance.

Relatives reported Tsolakis was a devoted husband and father who wouldn't have abandoned his family.

An online search indicated Tsoakis may be alive and living in Lake Hiawatha, New Jersey.

Tsolakis's relatives in Connecticut, Florida, and Greece reported that they never heard from Tsolakis after his disappearance.

Jeffery G. Dash

Missing: March 04, 1993

Stamford, Connecticut

DOB: February 20, 1969

Dash is a 24-year-old African American male, 5-09" tall, 217 Pounds, with black hair, brown eyes, and a scar on his right hand.

Dash was last seen in Stamford, Connecticut. Dash's abandoned vehicle was found on Route I-95 in New Rochelle, New York, with bloodstains in the car's interior.

Cyrus J. Quinn

Missing: August 14, 1993

Waterford, Connecticut

DOB: March 1950

Quinn is a 43-year-old white male 6-02" tall, 185 pounds, with brown hair, hazel eyes, a beard, and a mustache.

Cyrus Quinn resided in Waterford, Connecticut. His family last saw Quinn in New York on June 01, 1993.

He left for vacation to Mallorca and was never heard from again.

Quinn's belongings except his camera and wallet were left at his vacation home.

Quinn worked as a language teacher at Mitchell College.

An online search suggests that Quinn may live in New York.

Omayra Velasquez

October 16, 1993

Bridgeport, Connecticut

DOB: February 05, 1972

Velasquez is a 21-year-old Hispanic female, 5-02" tall, 150 pounds, with brown hair and brown eyes.

Velasquez was last seen wearing light-colored jeans, a short brown leather jacket, and black boots.

Velasquez was last seen on October 16, 1993, at approximately 8:00 am at her residence on Taylor Drive in Bridgeport, Connecticut.

Velasquez may have gone to a nightclub (George Star Cafe) on Iranistan Avenue.

Velasquez's brother Adam Velasquez said, "His sister had finished high school, and she had plans."

Velasquez was never seen again.

August M. Thiede (aka Bill)

Missing: June 10, 1994

Norfolk, Connecticut

DOB: December 15, 1909

Thiede is an 84-year-old (deceased) white male 5-08" tall, 150 pounds, with gray hair, hazel eyes, and missing his right pinky finger.

Thiede may have suffered from memory loss. Thiede was last seen wearing a brown vinyl jacket, blue jeans, a black baseball cap with "Elvis Presley" on it, and gray shoes.

Thiede was last seen at 8:45 am on June 10, 1994, in his yard at 998 Litchfield Road in Norfolk, Connecticut. Thiede was reported missing six hours after his disappearance. Thiede served in WWII from 1943-to 1946.

Thiede was last observed putting garbage in the back of his pick-up truck; he would bring the trash to the dump. Thiede's pick-up truck was parked at his residence; the pick-up truck keys were found in Thiede's house. Thiede may have attempted to travel to Maine to visit relatives. Thiede had lived in Fort Kent, Maine, in 1988. Thiede's daughter Pam Proctor also resides in Maine.

None of Thiede's credit cards or bank accounts showed any activity.

Jerry Dolphin

Missing: October 1994

New Haven, Connecticut

DOB: August 21, 1974

Dolphin is a 20-year-old African American male, 5-11" tall, 180 pounds, with black hair and brown eyes.

Dolphin was last seen in New Haven, Connecticut, in October 1994. On August 21, 1994, at 2:30 pm (Two months before Dolphin's disappearance), Gladys Punch and her brother Warren Tarkington were shot to death in Saint Lawrence Cemetery on Derby Street during an attempted robbery.

Dolphin may have witnessed the shooting and was murdered to ensure his silence. It was uncharacteristic for Dolphin not to stay in contact with his family.

Edivano Ribeiro

Missing: February 10, 1996

Danbury, Connecticut

DOB: November 10, 1971

Ribeiro is a 24-year-old Hispanic male, 5-07" tall, 150 pounds, with black hair and brown eyes.

Ribeiro was employed as a busboy and was last seen at his residence at 22 New Street in Danbury, Connecticut.

Ribeiro disappeared before a scheduled trip to visit his family in Brazil. It was not like Ribeiro to stay out of contact with family members; his vehicle was abandoned in a New York parking garage two years after his disappearance.

Kelley Zanon

Missing: February 08, 1996

Danbury, Connecticut

DOB: Unknown

Zanon is a Hispanic female, 5-07" tall, 130 pounds, with black hair, brown eyes, pierced ears, and a spider tattoo on her left shoulder.

On February 08, 1996, Zanon was last seen on Downs Street in Danbury, Connecticut.

No other information about Zanon's disappearance is available.

April Dawn Pennington

Missing: May 29, 1996

Montville, Connecticut

DOB: August 22, 1980

Pennington is a 15-year-old white female, 5-02" tall, 100 pounds, with brown hair, hazel eyes, a birthmark on her right arm, and pierced ears.

Pennington was last seen at her home on Orchard Drive in Montville, Connecticut, on May 29, 1996.

Pennington had climbed out through her brother's bedroom window and planned to meet with friends; one of the friends was later identified as George Leniart.

Her mother discovered her daughter missing at 5:30 am the following day when she went to wake April up for school. The window was left open, and a stuffed animal was tucked under her bed.

Leniart was incarcerated for raping a 13-year-old female. Leniart had told another inmate he had killed Pennington.

In 2008 inmate George Leniart was arrested for the murder of April Pennington.

The murder conviction was overturned.

Rosa Marie Camacho (aka Rosita)

Missing: October 24, 1997

Hartford, Connecticut

DOB: June 07, 1993

Camacho is a Hispanic female, 3-0" tall, 38 pounds, with brown hair and brown eyes. Camacho only spoke Spanish at the time of her disappearance. Camacho was last seen wearing a black jacket and blue pants.

Camacho and her mother, Rosa Delgado, left their home at approximately 5:00 pm to walk to a local store on Madison Avenue to buy groceries.

Delgado had left her 5-month-old daughter with her sister before leaving for the grocery store with Camacho.

When Delgado and Camacho disappear, Julio Camacho, Delgado's ex-boyfriend, was employed as a Hartford police officer.

Julio Camacho had been married when he began dating 16-year-old Delgado; he was also paying child support for three children from other relationships.

A witness observed Delgado speaking with her ex-boyfriend Julio J. Camacho near a street corner in Hartford's Parkville section.

In November of 1997, Delgado's body was found floating in a shallow section of Columbia Lake in the western part of New Jersey. At the time, her unidentified body was referred to as "The Lady of the Lake," and her body had been dismembered.

Julio Camacho had asked his brother to provide a false alibi after Delgado and Camacho's disappearance.

Julio Camacho
Officer

When authorities checked the trunk of Camacho's vehicle weeks later, they discovered the trunk liner had been removed, and the trunk's bottom had been sanded down. Authorities recovered a handmade hatch, wire garrote, and two sawed-off shotguns in the trunk. All the evidence had been thoroughly cleaned.

Two other women reported that while Camacho was in uniform, he had abducted, handcuffed, and raped them; five other women had come forward with similar allegations against Camacho.

In 1989 Julio Camacho was charged with third-degree assault of his ex-wife, Camacho was terminated from the police department, but he was later reinstated after the charges were dropped. Camacho resigned from the police department and later pleaded guilty to two rape charges. Camacho was released from prison and now resides in Virginia. It was also suggested that one of Camacho's former ex-wives could have been a suspect in the homicide.

Rosa Delgado's homicide and Rosa Camacho's disappearance remain unsolved.

Otava Radek

Missing: March 23, 1998

Middletown, Connecticut

DOB: 1973

Radek is a 24-year-old white male, 5-10" tall, 170 pounds, with brown hair and brown eyes. He speaks very little English.

Radek was last seen wearing a black t-shirt, a black coat with red stripes, and white pants.

On March 23, 1998, Radek was last seen in Middletown, Connecticut. He was last known to be driving a gray 1985 Plymouth Reliant.

Steven Raymond

Missing: July 28, 1998

New Britain, Connecticut

DOB: May 02, 1951

Raymond is a 47-year-old white male, 5-08" tall, 165 pounds, with brown hair, hazel eyes, and a scar on the left shoulder.

Raymond was last seen wearing a blue button-down long-sleeved shirt with a dark blue shirt-t with the word "Alert" in yellow lettering and black sneakers.

Raymond has a history of mental illness; he takes antidepressants and pain medication. Raymond was last seen near the intersection of South Street and Stanley Street in New Britain, Connecticut.

Raymond had planned on sleeping in a vacant area along South Street at the time of his disappearance. Raymond's sleeping bag and other personal property were found on South Street, where Raymond had planned to sleep.

Raymond lived with his parents until they moved into a smaller one-bedroom apartment on Chestnut Street.

Raymond began staying at the Salvation Army and the Friendship Center and eventually started sleeping outside on South Street

Raymond continued to visit his parents and eat breakfast and dinner at the Friendship Center.

Raymond had applied for municipal housing but was denied; he was angry about this but not depressed or suicidal.

Raymond was last seen on July 28, 1998.

Sandra Santiago

Missing: September 27, 1998

Hartford, Connecticut

DOB: November 17, 1968

Santiago is a 29-year-old white female 5-04" tall, 100 pounds, with brown hair, brown eyes, and pierced ears. It was reported that Santiago had needle marks (tracks) on her arms.

Santiago was last seen at the El Comerieno Café on Walnut Street in Hartford, Connecticut.

Santiago arrived at the club alone at approximately 9:00 pm.

Santiago failed to appear in court on a breach of peace charge. Her family said it was unlike Santiago to miss a court date.

Santiago left four children, three of her sons in foster care, and the daughter lives with relatives.

Brenda Roberts

Missing: April 24, 1999

Hartford, Connecticut

DOB: 1964

Roberts is a 35-year-old African American female, 5-01" tall, 140 pounds, with black hair and brown eyes. Roberts has scars on her right hand, right arm, head, and the left side of her face.

Roberts was last seen wearing a black t-shirt, a black jacket with red stripes, and white pants.

On April 24, 1999, Roberts was last seen in Hartford, Connecticut.

Frank Nash (aka Frank Asselin)

Missing: May 20, 1999

New Fairfield, Connecticut

DOB: April 15, 1964

Nash is a 35-year-old white male, 6-0" tall, 190 pounds, with brown hair and hazel eyes.

Nash had changed his birth name from Asselin to Nash; he may be wearing eyeglasses and blue jeans.

His father last saw Nash at his New Fairfield home on May 20, 1999.

On May 21, 1999, Nash called his father from the Danbury Department of Motor Vehicles, asking questions about his vehicle registration.

On June 3, 1999, Nash's 1994 Dodge Ram van displaying Connecticut license plate 770-CWV was abandoned. It was towed and impounded by the Salt Lake City, Utah, Sheriff's Department.

Nash's parents received notification of the van's recovery on June 06, 1999, at which time a missing person report was filed.

James Garris

Missing: July 07, 1999

Litchfield, Connecticut

DOB: February 24, 1919

Garris is a 98-year-old white male, 5-09" tall, 165 pounds, bald, with hazel eyes.

Garris was last seen wearing a short-sleeve white polo shirt, tan pants, and brown shoes. Garris has dementia.

Garris retired from Pratt and Whitney aircraft in 1978 and resided at the Sarah Pierce Assisted Living Community at 19 Constitution Way in Litchfield, Connecticut.

Garris was last seen at 6:00 am. Authorities believe he became confused and walked away from the premises; the temperature was in the mid-nineties when he disappearance.

Staff members reported Garris missing on July 07, 1999, at 8:50 pm. Garris moved into the assisted living facility four days before his disappearance.

It's thought Garris was attempting to make his way back to his old residence at 26 Elizabeth Street in Granby, Connecticut.

Andrea Michelle Reyes (aka Andrea Michelle Tenorio and Andrea Michelle Tenorio Reyes)

Missing: October 05, 1999

New Haven, Connecticut

DOB: November 09, 1997

Reyes is a 1-year-old Hispanic female, 3-0" tall, with black hair, brown eyes, a birthmark on the forehead, and a lazy right eye.

Reyes was last seen wearing blue jean overalls with purple pockets, a pink jacket with cartoon characters (Winnie the Pooh) on it, and pink and white sneakers. Reyes might have a medical condition.

It is believed that her non-custodial mother, Rose Tenorio, abducted Reyes. A felony warrant for custodial interference was issued for Tenorio in December 1999.

Tenorio may have left the United States and could be residing in Pueblo, Mexico.

There have been possible sightings in New Jersey and Hartford, Connecticut, but none of these reported sightings have been substantiated.

Bernadine Paul (aka Bernie)

Missing; June 07, 2000

Waterbury, Connecticut

DOB: November 12, 1962

Paul is a 37-year-old Hispanic female, 5-04" tall, 120 pounds, with brown hair, brown eyes, and pierced ears. Paul has moles on her upper lip and neck. Paul speaks fluent Spanish and has a cross tattoo between his left thumb and index finger.

Paul was last seen wearing a burgundy shirt, light blue jeans, a white jacket, two Bangle bracelets, two gold bracelets, a large silver bracelet, four rings, a gold chain with a cross pendant, and a black purse.

Before her disappearance, Paul let her friend borrow her car. Her friend then dropped Paul off at the Bradlees department store.

Paul was last seen at 3:15 pm in front of the Bradlees department store on Chase Avenue in Waterbury, Connecticut; she had withdrawn thirty dollars from the store's ATM.

12-14 hours later, Paul's friend contacted her mother because she had not heard from Paul.

Kevin John Belknap

Missing: April 08, 2001

Stonington, Connecticut

DOB: May 24, 1950

Belknap is a 50-year-old white male, 5-10" tall, 185 pounds, with brown hair and brown eyes.

Balknap was last seen wearing a long sleeve shirt, dark-colored "Docker" pants, black socks, black shoes, and a wristwatch.

Belknap was last seen on April 08, 2001, at approximately 5:00 pm at his residence at 20 Cutler Street in Stonington, Connecticut.

Belknap's blue 1998 Buick-LaSabre was abandoned in the Watch Hill coastal village in Westerly, Rhode Island. Belknap's work uniform was still in his vehicle.

Belknap's wife reported him missing on April 12, 2001, four days after his disappearance.

Belknap was employed as a blackjack (card game) dealer at the Foxwoods Resort Casino in Mashantucket, Connecticut.

Bianca Elaine Lebron

Missing: November 07, 2001

Bridgeport, Connecticut

DOB: June 21, 1991

Lebron is a 10-year-old Hispanic female, 4-11" tall, 115 pounds, with brown hair, hazel eyes, and a birthmark on her forehead.

Lebron was last seen wearing a green camouflage shirt, beige pants, black boots, and a dark blue denim jacket.

On November 07, 2001, Lebron entered the Elias Howe School on Clinton Avenue in Bridgeport, Connecticut.

Lebron told her classmates and teacher she was going shopping with her uncle that morning.

Lebron invited other classmates to go shopping with her, but the other classmates declined. At approximately 8:30 am, witnesses reported Lebron got into an older model two-tone (brown/beige) colored van with tinted windows.

Witnesses describe the van's operator as a 20 to 30-year-old medium-built Hispanic male, 5-08", with short-cropped curly black hair, brown eyes, long sideburns, a beard, and scratches on both cheeks.

The suspect was last seen wearing a long-sleeve pullover shirt with the word "Gap" on the front of the shirt and on both sleeves, "Fubu" jeans with a cartoon picture of "Fat Albert" on the back-right pants pocket, and beige Timberland boots.

(Similar Vehicle Used in Abduction)

At the time of the disappearance, Lebron's classmates believed the van's operator was her uncle. However, Lebron's mother reported Bianca did not have an uncle, and none of their family members owned a van.

Lebron lived with her mother, Carmelita Torres, and her stepfather Angelo Garcia.

It was thought that Bianca had not returned home from school and had gone to a friend's house. When Lebron did not return home by 8:30 pm that night, her mother contacted the authorities.

In November 2002, authorities wanted to question an acquaintance of Lebron's 20-year-old Jason Lara (aka Jason Gonzalez). However, Lara had moved to Fort Myers, Florida, a month after Lebron's disappearance.

At the time, Lara had been dating a 53-year-old woman who told police if anything ever happened to her, "Jason did it."

The woman said she believed Lara was capable of violence, and before Labron's disappearance, she heard Lara telling a friend he wanted a younger woman.

152

(Jason Lara)   (Suspect Sketch)

Lara was arrested on an unrelated second-degree forgery warrant (Giving a false name on a fingerprint card). Lara was then extradited to Bridgeport, Connecticut.

Lara had similar facial features to the suspect's composite drawing; Lara's friend owned a van identical to the van used in the abduction.

Several months after the van's disappearance was taken out of state and salvaged (crushed).

Lebron's great aunt Nancy Reboira said, "We think they got the right person; he looks like the guy in the sketch."

Lara had been incarcerated on several occasions, but he was out of prison at the time of Lebron's disappearance.

Authorities cleared Lara as a person of interest; however, the author disagrees with the decision.

Lebron's relative said Lara was Lebron's secret boyfriend, and Lebron was seen kissing Lara.

Lebron's grandmother said, "Bianca knew him (Lara); she often went to his house, but I don't think they were dating. She is too little a baby to be dating."

Lara's fiancé Corey Vitto said the allegation of Lara being Lebron's secret boyfriend was false, and the accusations started because of a feud between the Lebron and Lara families.

Vitto said she saw Lebron a few times during the summer before the girl disappeared, but she had been with Lara when he was with the girl. In 2009 authorities following a lead, authorities began excavating several broad areas of Seaside Park, but Lebron's body was never found.

Lebron's family still lives in Bridgeport, Connecticut. Lebron's father, Wilberto Lebron, now lives in Florida. Wilberto said he does not let his three children walk to school or take the bus; he drives them.

Wilberto said he would not allow his children to go on specific school field trips, and his children live a solitary lifestyle because of what happened to his daughter.

Lebron's mother had her daughter legally declared dead to file legal proceedings against the Bridgeport Board of Education for their negligence associated with Lebron's disappearance.

Lebron's mother's family is no longer cooperating with authorities.

Lebron's family believes, "There's somebody that knows something."

Like some of the other missing person cases, the suspect vehicle was released by the police and later salvaged (crushed) in an attempt to destroy forensic evidence.

Sherif Gewily

Missing: December 09, 2001

Meriden, Connecticut

DOB: March 11, 1998

Gewily is a 3-year-old white male with brown hair and brown eyes. Gewily speaks both English and Arabic.

Gewily is a citizen of both the United States and Egypt.

Gewily was last seen wearing an olive-green sweater, brown corduroy pants, and a blued hooded Blue Cross jacket.

Gewily was last seen in Meriden, Connecticut, on December 09, 2001. It is believed that Gewily may be in Egypt.

Jeffery L. Stone

Missing: January 30, 2003

Glastonbury, Connecticut

DOB: 1958

Stone is a 45-year-old white male, 5-09" tall, 160 Pounds, with brown hair and brown eyes. Stone has a reported history of medical problems.

Stone was last seen in Glastonbury, Connecticut on January 30, 2003.

No other information about Stone is available.

Israel Rosado

Missing: May 13, 2004

Bristol, Connecticut

DOB: September 13, 1983

Rosado is a 20-year-old Hispanic male, 5-06" tall. One hundred forty-five pounds, brown hair, brown eyes, and a birthmark on his neck and chin.

Rosado was last seen at 2:00 pm by his girlfriend at their Race Street apartment in Bristol, Connecticut; Rosado returned from a court appearance.

Rosado's girlfriend reported Rosado had made a telephone call to an unknown person; he (Rosado) then walked outside the house and entered a pick-up truck operated by an unidentified driver.

Rosado's cell phone service was canceled on the day of his disappearance. Rosado was a known drug trafficker making weekly trips between Waterbury, Connecticut, and the Bronx in New York.

Rosado kept in close contact with his mother, contacting her several times a week, he has not been heard from since the day of his disappearance, and foul play is suspected.

Evelyn Ann Frisco (aka Evy)

Missing: June 29, 2004

New Haven, Connecticut

DOB: May 04, 1962

Frisco is a 42-year-old white female, 5-02" tall, 125 pounds, with brown hair, blue eyes, upper denture plate, scar on right leg, "Gemini" tattoo on the right ankle, a symbol of the rose, butterfly, sunset, and the name "Phil" on her right shoulder.

Medical conditions include hepatitis and cirrhosis of the liver.

Frisco was wearing jeans, and black shoes and possibly carrying a black pocketbook.

Frisco was last seen during a court appearance for shoplifting in New Haven, Connecticut. Frisco was released on a two-year conditional discharge.

Frisco was a known prostitute and drug abuser; she was also a police informant at the time of her disappearance.

Frisco's mother, Janet Frisco, believed someone wanted to hurt her daughter based on an earlier conversation in 2004 when her daughter said, "Mom, can I have some money? I think this is my last birthday."

Frisco's mother did not report her missing until later in 2004 because she thought her daughter was in jail.

Frisco also knew Lisa Calvo, another woman who disappeared in New Haven, Connecticut. Frisco and Calvo had a lengthy criminal history of prostitution and drug abuse.

The authorities do not believe the Frisco or the Calvo case is connected, nor do they think the girls met with foul play.

The author believes the cases are linked, and both victims had met with foul play.

Ande Fan (aka Andy or Andre)

Missing: August 08, 2004

New Haven, Connecticut

DOB: March 21, 1973

Fan is a 31-year-old Asian male, 5-04" tall, 180 pounds, with black hair and brown eyes.

Fan is bipolar and suffers from other medical conditions.

Fan was last seen at his residence at the Bella Vista apartments at 339 Eastern Street in New Haven, Connecticut. All of Fan's personal property, including his keys, money, passport, and other identification, was left behind in his apartment.

The Fair Haven neighborhoods surrounding the Belle Vista apartments are crime-infested. Fan regularly contacted family members; there has been no activity with any of Fan's banking accounts. Fan talked about returning to China. However, there is no evidence suggesting he left the United States.

Fan suffered from mental illness, but staff members at Bella Vista apartments reported that Fan did not seem troubled or despondent before his disappearance. A Bella Vista apartment coordinator identified as Corrine Reveux reported seeing Fan with an unidentified black male before his disappearance.

160

William Paul Smolinski Jr.

Missing: August 24, 2004

Waterbury, Connecticut

DOB: January 14, 1973

Smolinski is a 31-year-old white male, 5-11" tall, 200 pounds, with brown hair, blue eyes, bowlegged, left pierced ear, a tattoo of a blue cross outlined in orange on his left shoulder, and a tattoo of a cross with the word "Pruitt" in the center of his right forearm.

Smolinski was last seen wearing a denim shirt, blue jeans, work boots, a diamond earring, and a gold rope necklace with a cross pendant. Smolinski was last seen at his residence on Holly Street in Waterbury, Connecticut. On the day of his disappearance, Smolinski told a neighbor he would look at a car and be gone for three days; he asked the neighbor if she could feed his dog while he was gone.

The neighbor said Smolinski never returned with his house keys. The neighbor reported last seeing Smolinski at approximately 3:30 pm. Smolinski's two vehicles were left behind at his residence. His wallet and keys were found inside one of the cars.

Smolinski worked full-time as an apprentice technician for Midland Heating and Air Conditioning. He also worked part-time for Durable Towing Service. Smolinski occasionally mowed lawns and plowed driveways during the winter.

After his disappearance, Smolinski's bank account and social security number were not used or accessed.

A person interested in the case was identified as Chad Hanson, a known convict, and drug addict. He told authorities that an individual identified as Shaun Karpiuk, another known drug addict, had beaten Smolinski to death with a hammer and wrapped his body in a carpet. Hanson reported helping Karpiuk bury Smolinski's body.

Before Smolinski's disappearance, Smolinski had dated Karpiuk's mother, Madeline Gleason. The couple separated because Smolinski believed Gleason was seeing another man.

Gleason told authorities Smolinski had been at her house the morning of the disappearance, and when he left, Smolinski appeared "A little depressed."

(Smolinski and Gleason)

Karpuik and Hanson were never charged with Smolinski's murder. At the time of Smolinski's disappearance, Gleason had been dating Christopher Sorenson. Sorenson told authorities that when Smolinski disappeared, he received a call from Smolinski. Smolinski told him, "Watch your back; at all times."

The last three telephone calls made by Smolinski were to Sorenson. Witnesses reported Hanson bragged about helping Karpiuk murder Smolinski. Hanson told people they would never find the body. In 2005, a person of interest, Shaun M. Karpiuk, died of a heroin overdose.

Robert P. Cavanaugh

Missing: December 24, 2004

Mansfield, Connecticut

DOB: January 03, 1953

Cavanaugh is a 51-year-old white man, 5-10" tall, 185 pounds, with brown hair, blue eyes, with a scar on his knee and shoulder. Cavanaugh has a history of depression.

Cavanaugh failed to show up for work on December 24, 2004; he was last seen at his house on Foster Drive in Willimantic, Connecticut.

He had left a note (contents unknown) at his home and drove away in his black 1996 Mazda B2300 pick-up truck displaying Connecticut license plate 681-CZT.

Family members reported Cavanaugh was despondent before leaving the house; he was last seen operating his vehicle on Stafford Road in Mansfield, Connecticut.

There are few details available concerning Cavanaugh's disappearance.

Bettina Diane Scott (aka Tina)

Missing: December 25, 2004

East Lyme, Connecticut

DOB: July 20, 1957

Scott is a 47-year-old white female, 5-05" tall, 110 pounds, with brown hair, brown eyes, and pierced ears, and she has a tracheotomy scar on her neck. Scott has an unspecified medical condition.

On December 25, 2004, Scott was last seen at a relative's residence on Boston Post Road and Highway Route 161 in East Lyme, Connecticut.

There was a possible sighting of Scott on Allen Place in Hartford, Connecticut, a couple of days after she was reported missing.

Robert F. Duerr

Missing: January 15, 2005

Waterford, Connecticut

DOB: 1964

Duerr is a 41-year-old white male, 5-10" tall, 175 pounds, with brown hair and brown eyes.

Duerr was last seen wearing a black leather jacket, a long blue sleeve sweatshirt, and gray sweatpants.

Duerr has diabetes.

On January 15, 2005, Duerr was last seen at approximately 1:00 am at the Fountain Care Center in Waterford, Connecticut.

The staff noticed Duerr missing at approximately 4:00 am. It is believed that Duerr walked away from the facility.

At the time of Duerr's disappearance, it was cold, and it had been reported that Deurr was not appropriately dressed for the cold weather.

Duerr's bank card was found in the Charter Oaks Federal Credit Union's night dropbox three days after his disappearance.

Foul play is not suspected in Duerr's disappearance.

Lisa Ann Calvo

Missing: October 06, 2005

New Haven, Connecticut

DOB: February 02, 1965

Calvo is a 40-year-old white female, 4-11" tall, 105 pounds, with brown hair, brown eyes, with a "Spider web" tattoo on her right thigh and leg.

Calvo was addicted to heroin and was in failing health at the time. She was homeless and living on the streets at the time of her disappearance. She had lost custody of her children and planned to sign herself into a drug treatment facility and move back into her parent's house in an attempt to regain custody of her children.

Calvo was last seen on the morning of her disappearance by family members.

Like Evelyn Frisco's disappearance in New Haven, Connecticut, Calvo maintained regular contact with her family. On the day of her disappearance, she asked her mother to wire her money for a scheduled court appearance. Authorities confirmed that Calvo had picked up the money even at 5:30 pm and was never seen again.

Calvo and Frisco had known each other. There were reported sightings of Calvo in the vicinity of Grand Avenue and Murray Place (past residence) in New Haven, Connecticut.

166

The authorities do not believe there is a connection between either the Calvo or Frisco disappearances. Both Calvo and Frisco are still considered missing.

The Connecticut State attorney's Office has offered a $50,000 reward for information in the case.

Jose Ortiz (aka Bin Laden)

Missing: December 28, 2005

New Haven, Connecticut

DOB: 1986

Ortiz is a 19-year-old Hispanic male, 5-11" tall, 140 pounds, with brown hair and brown eyes.

Ortiz was last seen wearing a black hooded sweatshirt and blue jeans. Ortiz was riding a bicycle at the time of his disappearance.

On the same day of Ortiz's disappearance, a New Haven firefighter witnessed three young males abduct a person riding a bicycle near the fire station located at Poplar and Lombard Street.

The three suspects were observed pulling the victim off the bicycle and forcing him into a gray 1990s Ford Taurus.

Authorities believed that Ortiz was involved in drug activity and was the victim of an abduction.

Within one year, Jose Ortiz (2005), Lisa Calvo (2005), and Evelyn Anna Frisco (2004) had gone disappeared in New Haven, Connecticut. All were suspected of being involved in illegal drug activity.

Antonio Gomez

Missing: March 13, 2006

Waterbury, Connecticut

DOB: 1950

Gomez is a 56-year-old Hispanic male, 5-06" tall, 185 pounds, with black hair and brown eyes.

On August 14, 2006, Gomez was last seen in Waterbury, Connecticut.

Gomez may have once resided in the Bronx, New York. It is believed that Gomez left Connecticut on his own accord.

Mark Randall Johnson

Missing: October 24, 2006

Tolland, Connecticut

DOB: August 11, 1964

Johnson is a 42-year-old white male, 5-10" tall, 170 pounds, with blond hair and blue eyes.

Johnson was last seen wearing a dark-colored sheepskin jacket, a long gray sleeve shirt, dark jeans, snow boots, and a baseball cap with "NY" on it. Medical condition (unspecified), Johnson may have been depressed over personal problems before his disappearance.

On October 24, 2006, Johnson was last seen at approximately 11:25 am, walking away from his residence on Cider Mill Road in Tolland, Connecticut.

It was uncharacteristic of Johnson to keep out of touch with his family. Johnson was married several months before his disappearance; his wife stated that he had called her several times after his disappearance. Johnson's wife, Donna-Lee Maheu-Senk, said she believes he left because he faced prison time for drug paraphernalia charges; he was also wanted for failing to appear in court stemming from the original possession of drug paraphernalia charge.

At the time, Johnson had violated the conditions of probation.

In October 2010, at the request of his sister Johnson was legally declared dead.

The case remains open.

Tamara Barriga

Missing: June 13, 2008

Waterbury, Connecticut

DOB: 1975

Barriga is a 33-year-old light-skinned Afro-American female, 5-03" tall, 140 pounds, with brown hair and brown eyes.

Barriga was last seen in Waterbury, Connecticut, on June 13, 2008. Barriga has a history of prostitution, but it is unclear if this had anything to do with her disappearance.

No other information is available.

Griselda Aguirre

Missing: July 30, 2008

Hartford, Connecticut

DOB: October 20, 1993

Aguirre is a 14-year-old Hispanic female, 5-04" tall, 140 pounds, with black hair and brown eyes.

Aguirre was last seen wearing a white t-shirt and white pants.

Aguirre was last seen in Hartford, Connecticut, on July 30, 2008; it is believed that Aguirre may be in Mexico and maybe in the company of an older adult male and a young child.

No other information is available on the case.

Awilda Marrero

Missing: April 06, 2009

Enfield, Connecticut

DOB: January 17, 1966

Marrero is a 43-year-old Hispanic female, 5-01" tall, 165 pounds, with brown hair and brown eyes. Marrero has a scar on her upper right arm, pierced ears, a tattoo with "Mike" on her left buttock, and the word "Joel" tattooed on her right knee and thigh.

Marrero was last seen wearing a nightgown, jeans, a brown jacket, and no shoes.

Marrero was seen by her daughter Angelica Carmona at 16 Asnuntuck Street in Enfield, Connecticut, at approximately 11:30 pm. Marrero left the house without taking her purse or cell phone or getting fully dressed.

The next day (April 07, 2009), Marrero's daughter said she woke up at 7:30 am and noticed her mother missing. Her daughter thought her mother had either gone for a walk or went fishing, but her daughter wondered why her mother did not take her shoes.

On the night before Marrero's disappearance, Marrero had told her daughter's boyfriend, "Take care of my daughter if anything happens to me."

Marrero took prescribed medication at the time of her disappearance (unknown medical or psychological condition).

Marrero's boyfriend was involved in illegal drug use, but he had been incarcerated at the time of her disappearance.

A K9 tracked Marrero from her residence to a boat launch on South River Street, bordering the Connecticut River.

This was where Marrero always went fishing; however, authorities believe the tracks may have been a few days old.

Carrie Ann Monroe

Missing: January 20, 2010

Berlin, Connecticut

DOB: 1984

Monroe is a 26-year-old white female who is 5-01" tall, 110 pounds, with brown hair, blue eyes, and pierced ears.

Monroe was seen wearing a black half jacket, blue jeans, and black sneakers with a red design.

Monroe was last seen at 3:30 am on January 20, 2010, at the Comfort Motel on the Berlin Turnpike in Berlin, Connecticut.

Monroe left the motel and traveled to an apartment on the south side of Hartford, Connecticut. Monroe had left several personal items at the condo in Hartford before her disappearance.

Monroe's boyfriend did not report her missing; he stated, "He thought she simply left on her own accord."

It was common for Monroe to disappear for several days; however, she always kept in contact with relatives or friends. Monroe's friends reported her missing nine days later.

Monroe was known to frequent Waterbury, Hartford, and New Haven, Connecticut.

Mery Acosta (aka Maricruz Acosta, Mery Raquel Acosta, Mery Acosta-Matia, and Mery Ramirez-Ceron)

Missing: June 06, 2011

Danbury, Connecticut

DOB: May 02, 1994

Acosta is a 17-year-old Hispanic female, 5-0" tall, 150 Pounds, with brown hair and brown eyes.

Acosta was last seen in Danbury, Connecticut, on June 06, 2011; authorities believe she left on her own accord. No other information on the case is available.

Marquita Jones (aka Luv, Quita, Keigha, or Kecia)

Missing: 2011

New Haven, Connecticut

DOB: 1983

Jones is a 28-year-old African American female, 5-02" tall, 100 pounds, with black hair and brown eyes.

Jones was last seen on West Street in the mid-summer of 2011. Jones has a history of substance abuse.

Jones might be living in the Hill section of New Haven, Connecticut.

No other information about Jones is available.

Angel Garcia (aka Ito)

Missing: October 21, 2011

Hartford, Connecticut

DOB: March 05, 1992

Garcia is a 19-year-old Hispanic male, 5-10" tall, 180 pounds, with brown hair, brown eyes, and a scar on the right knuckle, right knee, and chin.

Garcia was last seen wearing a gray hooded sweatshirt, blue jeans, and black sneakers with a red design.

Garcia was last seen operating a red Honda 85cc dirt bike with a large yellow "Geico" logo on the side.

The dirt bike was possibly stolen from a local motorcycle gang member; Garcia was operating the dirt bike in a wooded area near New Britain and Newfield Avenue.

Garcia was riding with a friend, and they became separated. Garcia was never seen again.

Garcia's father (Ralph Garcia) said, "Someone was chasing him, some guys in a gray Jeep-Cherokee."

There has been no activity on Garcia's cell phone or bank accounts.

(Red Dirt Bike)

It is most likely one of the individuals (motorcycle gang members) in the gray Jeep-Cherokee owned the stolen dirt bike, which is why Garcia met with foul play.

Unidentified Bodies in Connecticut

Jane Doe (aka Lorraine Stahl)

Date Found: May 30, 1974

1313UFCT (Doe Network)

On May 30, 1974, an unidentified white female, 25 to 30 years old, 5-04' to 5-05' tall, 100-110 pounds with brown or auburn hair, was found wrapped in a blanket in a shallow grave behind a house located at 139 Shewville Road in the town of Ledyard, Connecticut.

The unidentified female remains were found wearing a beige leather vest, gold-beige sweater, brown skirt, brown knee-high granny boots, and a yellow raincoat. The victim died of a single gunshot wound to the head.

The shallow grave also contained the body of Stahl's boyfriend Gustavous Lee Carmichael Jr., 22, a known bank robber and an escaped prisoner.

The unidentified female had a 1917 fraternity or sorority ring with the letters "JHNS" or "JNHS" impressed outside the ring. The ring contained the initials "ILN" on the inside.

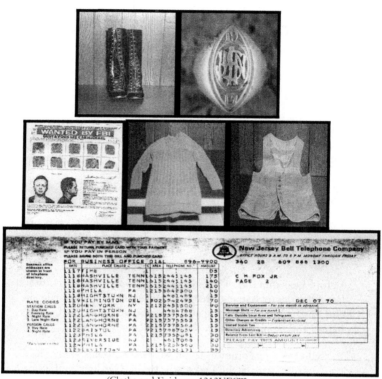

(Cloths and Evidence 1313UFCT)

The 1917 ring is a fraternity or sorority ring manufactured by the L. G. Balfour Company in Attleboro, Massachusetts. Balfour began manufacturing college rings in 1913 and did not make high school rings until 1922. The ring belonged to Stahl's grandparents or was taken during a heist involving Stahl.

The victim's possessions also included a New Jersey Bell telephone bill showing a list of telephone numbers she had called.

She had made calls to Tennessee (Nashville), Pennsylvania (Philadelphia, Langhorne, Bristol, and Levittown), New Jersey (Hightstown, Riverside, Caldwell, Allentown, Burlington, and from Neward), Delaware (Wilmington), and New York (New York City and Buffalo).

Stahl was observed as a passenger in a 1964 green Oldsmobile with Maine license plates; the vehicle was later found dumped in Hartford, Connecticut.

The vehicle more than likely belonged to or was stolen by Carmichael's associate and fellow bank robber, Roger Wayne Brown, age 22 (Federal Inmate #01017-084), who had once lived in Lewiston, Maine.

Authorities believe Carmichael had only known Stahl for a short time before they were murdered.

Stahl may have been working in New York before meeting Carmichael.

Before December 31, 1970, Stahl had told DeFreitas's common-law wife Joanne Rainello that she was afraid of the lifestyle she and Carmichael were living and was worried about using false names and being caught by the police.

Rainello told her common-law-husband DeFreitas about the conversation with Stahl. DeFreitas, Brant, Gardner, and Rainello were concerned about the threat that Stahl posed.

The group concluded there was too much at stake, so they decided to lure Carmichael and Stahl to the Shewville house and murder them.

On December 31, 1970, Carmichael and Stahl arrived at the Shewville Road home, and after arguing, Stahl threatened to go to the police. At that point, DeFreitas shot Carmichael multiple times, killing him. Brant then shot Stahl in the head.

The bodies were placed on a sled and moved to an area of the property bordering a small brook; reports indicate it had been too cold to dig a deep grave, so the bodies were placed in a shallow grave.

Carmichael, DeFreitas, James Gardner, Donald Brant, and William Royce were responsible for a string of bank robberies which extended throughout New England from the late 1960s and 1970s.

State v. DeFreitas

179 Conn. 431 (1980)

STATE OF CONNECTICUT v. RICHARD DEFREITAS

Supreme Court of Connecticut.

Argued October 4, 1979.

The bodies of a man and a woman were buried in a shallow grave in a wooded area behind an A-frame house on Shewville Road in Ledyard, Connecticut. They were recovered by the Connecticut State Police on May 30, 1974, acting on information supplied by Joanne Rainello, formerly the defendant's common-law wife.

An autopsy determined that the man had died from gunshot wounds to the head and chest and that the woman had died from a single gunshot wound to her head and brain.

On November 12, 1974, a grand jury found an actual bill of indictment charging the defendant with two counts of murder in the first degree in violation of General Statutes 53-9 (now 53a-54a).

After that, a petit jury of twelve returned a guilty verdict on both counts of the indictment as to the defendant Richard DeFreitas and his codefendant Donald Brant, now deceased.

The defendant's motion to set aside the verdict was denied, judgment was entered, and the defendant appealed.

The defendant has primarily raised two claims of error on appeal.

To fully understand the nature of the claims and their factual and legal underpinnings, it is necessary to delineate the facts that a jury might reasonably find the evidence introduced at trial would link the defendant with the murders.

The dead male body discovered in the shallow grave on May 30, 1974, was subsequently identified by dental records as Gustavus Lee Carmichael; the female body's identity was never established.

On October 5, 1970, Carmichael and another man escaped from a deputy United States marshal while being transported from a Massachusetts state prison to federal court in Hartford to be sentenced for charges then pending against them.

Carmichael and the other man robbed a New Jersey bank on December 22, 1970, of approximately $60,000.

Escaping Men Handcuff Two

WINDSOR, Conn. (AP) :— Two federal marshals and a prisoner were overpowered and handcuffed to a tree Monday by two federal prisoners who were being taken to U.S. District Court in Hartford for sentencing on bank robbery charges.

Police put out a statewide alert for the pair, who fled in the marshals' car with one of the marshals' .38-caliber revolvers.

State police said the marshals and the third prisoner were not injured. They said the two fugitives were considered dangerous and anyone sighting the car should not approach it.

The escapees were identified as Gustavous Lee Carmichael, 23, Boston, and Roger Joseph Brown, 24, Lewiston, Maine.

(Carmichael Escaped)

Carmichael and a woman companion (the other murder victim) six days later, on December 28, 1970, appeared at the A-frame Ledyard home of the defendant DeFreitas and his common-law wife, Joanne. They were living there under the names of Ray and Joanne Emerson.

On that date, the defendant, DeFreitas, returned to his Ledyard home after committing a bank robbery in Newport, Rhode Island, where he had stolen approximately $30,000. By his admission, DeFreitas was a professional thief and robber.

Among the defendant's criminal associates were the other defendant Donald Brant, now deceased, and James Gardner. They, along with Joanne Rainello, offered the crucial testimony linking the defendants DeFreitas and Brant to the murder of Carmichael and his companion Lorianne Stahl.

Brant and Gardner were at DeFreitas's home on December 28, 1970. In the presence of Carmichael and his woman companion, DeFreitas divided the $30,000 spoils from his robbery with Brant and Gardner.

DeFreitas stated that the three were partners and that they should take care of each other. When one of the three would commit a robbery, they would share the proceeds; the trio possessed several weapons in their arsenal and maintained some apartments around Providence where they would harbor criminals.

Carmichael and his companion came to Ledyard while running from the police. They were seeking a place to hide out. They stayed two nights at the DeFreitas home, and DeFreitas provided them with false identity papers in Dirk and Lorraine Stahl's names, who had once been residents of the same inn as the defendant.

He had appropriated some of their identification documents. Carmichael's woman companion opened a checking account under the name of Lorraine Stahl, and on December 30, 1970, the couple moved to a home they had rented in Noank under the name of Stahl.

At the time, Carmichael's female companion, who was now using the name Lorraine Stahl, was at DeFreita's home in Ledyard. She expressed fears to Joanne Rainello about her life and told Rainello she was nervous about using fictitious names and was afraid of being caught by the police. Rainello relayed this information to DeFreitas.

At this point, the defendant called Donald Brant at his home in Rhode Island to discuss the threat Carmichael, and his female companion posed.

DeFreitas and Brant decided to kill Gustavus Carmichael and his female companion because DeFreitas and Brant concluded they had too much at stake and considered Carmichael and his girlfriend a threat. They could not kill her without killing him as well.

After making plans to carry out murders, DeFreitas lured the victims back to his A-frame house on Shewville Road in Ledyard on December 31, 1970.

The defendant shot Carmichael repeatedly and killed him; Brant shot and killed the woman. The defendant and Brant described how the shootings had taken place to Joanne Rainello and James Gardner.

Rainello was out of the house at the time of the murders and was picked up later by DeFreitas. Shortly after the murders, DeFreitas called Gardner to come to the Ledyard house because of a "problem."

When he arrived at the A-frame house, Gardner was told for the first time that DeFreitas and Brant had murdered Carmichael and his female companion.

The reason given to Gardner for the murders was that DeFreitas and Brant feared Carmichael's female companion would tell the police everything if the police caught her.

In his appeal, the defendant's first claim is that the trial court excluded the testimony of three witnesses called by the defense to testify about alleged third-party declarations against penal interest.

The defendant contends that these declarations were inconsistent with the guilt of the defendant. Thus, their exclusion deprived him of his due process right to a fair trial in violation of the United States constitution's fourteenth amendment.

The three witnesses called by the defense purportedly were to testify as to five declarations concerning the murders in question in the present case, which were allegedly made by the following third-party declarants: James Gardner and Joanne Rainello, both of whom had earlier in the trial been called to testify by the prosecution and who was testifying under a grant of immunity by the state, and one John Robichaud, who had died before the trial.

The first of these witnesses, Thomas A. Greene, called by the defense, testified that he was then serving a sentence for robbery, and in the previous fifteen to twenty years, he had had many felony convictions.

He also testified that he had known James Gardner for about fourteen years, and Gardner was the best man at his wedding on December 7, 1970.

When Greene started to testify about a conversation with Gardner two and one-half weeks after the wedding, the state's attorney objected. In the jury's absence, the defendant's trial counsel offered proof of the content of two conversations between Gardner and Greene. In the first conversation, Gardner allegedly requested Greene to kill a man and a woman in Connecticut.

In the second conversation, which was supposed to have taken place in early January 1971, Greene asked Gardner whether he had been "kidding" about the request in the first conversation. Gardner allegedly replied that the matter had been taken care of by Gardner and another person named Gardner and was not either of the defendants on trial.

Besides, the defendant's attorney advised the court to admit the testimony since it bore a marked identity to the offense being tried. Therefore, there was a suggestion that Gardner might have very well committed the crime.

The next witness called by the defense was Gerald Mastracchio.

He testified that he was serving a life sentence for robbery and murder and had a substantial felony record for over thirty years. He knew James Gardner and one John Robichaud, having been incarcerated in the Adult Correctional Institution in Cranston, Rhode Island. Robichaud, at the time of the trial, was deceased.

As Mastracchio was about to testify to an alleged conversation with Robichaud concerning Carmichael, one of the victims in this case, and a young woman, presumably the other victim, the state's attorney objected, and again the jury was excused. The defense's offer of proof was that Mastracchio would testify that Robichaud had told Mastracchio that Gardner and Robichaud had murdered Carmichael and the young woman and buried their bodies.

192

Before being excused as a witness, Mastracchio indicated to the trial court that he would like to testify further. In the jury's absence, he was permitted to relate the contents of those further statements.

Mastracchio testified that he had once spoken with Joanne Rainello in the Adult Correction Institute's visiting room in Rhode Island sometime in the 1970s when Richard DeFreitas was present.

At that meeting, she allegedly asked Mastracchio if he could get in touch with John Robichaud. She feared Robichaud because she had participated in the murder with him and Gardner. Rainello reportedly indicated that she had lured Carmichael and his female companion over to the house so that Robichaud and Gardner could kill them. Although Mastracchio's proffered testimony was excluded, the defendant DeFreitas testified about this alleged conversation on redirect examination.

The state's objection to his testimony was withdrawn when the claim was made that it was offered to attack Rainello's credibility and to show bias. Devlin testified that while traveling with Robichaud and another man in early 1971, Robichaud told him that he and a man from Rhode Island named Jimmy had killed Carmichael.

Devlin did not recall any mention of a woman being involved in that episode, and he stated that Robichaud was no longer alive and that he had been killed (Justia, US Law).

The next witness called by the defense was Richard Devlin, who testified in the jury's absence that he was in a Massachusetts prison serving time on a manslaughter charge. He knew Carmichael and Robichaud because they had spent time with him in prison.

193

(Cornelia Enright)   (Ikonka Cann}

April 24, 1969   May 24, 1969
Rotterdam, NY.   Huntington Mills, PA.
18 years old   22 years old
Height: 5-02'   Height 5-06'
Weight: 115 lbs.   Weight: 122-130
Hair Color: Straw   Hair: Blonde
Eye Color: Blue   Eye: Blue

To date, Stahl's real name is unknown.

CONN. POLICE SEEKING INFO ON HOMICIDE VICTIM

Connecticut State Police are seeking information about the identity of one victim in a 1970 double homicide whose remains were uncovered in Ledyard, CT, May 30, 1974. The other victim was identified as Gustavus Lee Carmichael, a former Boston resident and fugitive from justice.

The unidentified victim, a 25-30 year old female, was 5'4" or 5'5" tall, weighed about 100 to 110 pounds, was of medium build, and had brownish red hair. She was last known to be working in New York City and is believed to have relatives living in Tennessee, West Virginia, or the Carolinas.

The unidentified female was wearing two rings and a wood-carved broach or pendant. One ring appears to be a school ring with the letters J.H.S.N. in monogram and the initials I.L.N. and the date 1917 engraved inside. The other ring is an inexpensive one with an imitation emerald stone. The wood-carved figure appears to be an abstract ceremonial head.

Anyone with information concerning the victim's identity is urged to reply to Detective Division, Conn. State Police Department, 100 Washington Street, Hartford, Conn. 06101 or call (area code 203) 566-2250.

(Unidentified Female)

195

John Doe – (Granby, Connecticut)

Date Found: September 04, 1977

214UMCT (Doe Network)

Granby, Connecticut

On September 04, 1977, an individual collecting walnut found the victim, a white male, face down Enders Road in Enders State Park in Granby, Connecticut.

The victim had died from blunt force trauma to the skull (skull fracture), his larynx, and facial bones (fractures). The authorities believe he was killed where he was found. It was estimated that the death occurred approximately twenty-four hours before his body was found. The victim is believed to be between 20 to 30 years old.

The victim was 5-07" tall, 140 pounds, with brown hair with blonde roots worn in a ponytail, a mole on the right ear, a scar on his right knee, two U-shaped scars on his upper left chest, a vaccination scar on his upper left arm, missing and chipped teeth. It has not been determined if the chipped teeth resulted from an assault.

The victim was wearing a white knotted long-sleeve shirt with a picture of a beige and green building with blue rectangles on it, a white t-shirt with the word "Ferguson" on it, and yellow "Levi" corduroy pants. The victim was not wearing any shoes or socks.

Jane Doe (West Haven, Connecticut)

Date Found: April 20, 1979

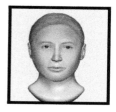

1196UFCT (Doe Network)

West Haven, Connecticut

(WestClox Watch)

On April 20, 1979, the partial skeletal remains of an unidentified white female, 18 to 30 years old, 5-03" tall, with a possible missing lower vertebra, were found on New Haven Water Company property bordering Route 34 in West Haven, Connecticut.

It is believed the victim died between 1971 and 1978.

The victim wore a black lace bra and a "WestClox" traveling watch in a red case.

Jane Doe (Westport, Connecticut)

Date Found: May 19, 1985

836UFCT (Doe Network)

Westport, Connecticut

On May 19, 1985, an unidentified Afro-American female, 30 to 40 years old, 5-0" tall, weighing 110 pounds, was found burning in a pile of tires in a wooded area off of the should of Route I-95 near the Sasco Creek overpass exit 19 in Westport, Connecticut, her hand and feet were dismembered.

The victim wore a wool wrap-around sweater, "Russler" blue jeans, and a bra with two safety pins as claps.

In a similar case, Bridgeport police found the woman's body in a vacant lot near Lafayette Street and Railroad Avenue on June 5, 1993. Her body was severely burned and unidentifiable. The woman was likely between 25 and 35 years old.

Jane Doe (New Britain, Connecticut)

Date Found: October 11, 1991

705UFCT (Doe Network)

New Britain, Connecticut

On October 11, 1991, an unidentified white or Hispanic female, 25 to 30 years old, 5-05" tall, weighing 135 pounds, with straight black hair, and a small tooth protruding from her mouth, was found near the railroad tracks on Myrtle Street in New Britain, Connecticut.

The victim had died from a gunshot wound to the head.

The victim wore a white sleeveless sundress and a shirt with "Panda Bears" on it. One Panda was holding a red ice cream cone, one was Panda holding a red umbrella, and the other Panda was holding a yellow heart with two Pandas holding each other.

In 1995 the body of 17-year-old Elizabeth Honsh was found behind a strip mall in New Britain. Honsh's mother, 53-year-old Marcia Honsh, was located near the entrance to Tolland State Park. Both died of a gunshot wound to the head.

Marcia Honsh's husband has been charged with their murders.

John Doe (Milford, Connecticut)

Date Found: August 21, 1992

1714UMCT (Doe Network)

Milford, Connecticut

On August 21, 1992, a couple walking in the woods along Oronoque Road discovered the victim's skeletal remains wrapped in a pink blanket, a green sheet, and two plastic garbage bags.

The victim died from four small-caliber gunshot wounds.

The authorities believe the victim was killed at a different location.

The victim was an Asian male, 18 to 30 years old, 5-06" tall, 130 pounds, with straight black hair.

The victim wore a long-sleeve button-down shirt with the word "Forever" on the left chest pocket, a V-neck t-shirt, denim pants, and a brown belt buckle with a yellow metal belt.

John Doe - (Old Saybrook, Connecticut)

Date Found: March 31, 1998

272UMCT (Doe Network)

Old Saybrook, Connecticut

On March 31, 1998, the unidentified male was found in a marsh area of the Connecticut River in Old Saybrook, Connecticut. The estimated time of death was from 1-5 years before being discovered.

The victim is believed to be a white or Hispanic male, 25 to 35 years old, 5-08" tall, and weighing an estimated 200 pounds. The victim had a broken nose.

The victim was wearing a black "Lavon" windbreaker with a maroon/purple zipper, size 9.5 "Fila" sneakers, and black "Levi 550" pants.

Other Unidentified Bodies in Connecticut

.

Unidentified Adult Male – The Shoe Box Murder

August 10, 1886

Wallingford, Connecticut

On August 8, 1886, while walking through the Parker farm district of Wallingford, Edward Turill and his dog found what appeared to be a crate of shoes that he believed had fallen from a cart. The box measured 12 inches by 30 inches long and was lying in a clump of low-lying bushes.

After removing the box's cover, Turill found the body of a man wrapped in tar paper, to his horror. The body was missing its head, legs, and arms.

The victim was a young male, perhaps in his thirties, 175 pounds. He had died about five to 10 days earlier. Further examination found in his stomach a large quantity of arsenic.

In September 1886, police recovered two human arms and legs near the scene. The limbs were also wrapped in tar paper like the torso found in the shoe box.

A woman identified as Mabel Gage came forward and reported to police that she knew the whole story behind the murder, but when asked to tell the story in court, Gage professed to know nothing.

Two years after the murder, Gage committed suicide.

The murder mystery captured the nation's attention, generating sensational headlines nationwide.

The New York Times ran a front-page article that characterized the murder as "One of the most brutal tragedies in the criminal annals of the State."

Despite all the national attention, the case hasn't produced credible leads. No other information about the victim or suspect's identity has ever surfaced.

Unidentified Infant – The Newspaper Baby

September 27, 1921

Enfield, Connecticut

On November 11, 1930, a construction worker demolishing a building on River Road in Enfield found a deceased baby wrapped in a newspaper inside one of the building's walls.

The newspaper was dated September 27, 1921. There were two possible reported causes of death; the baby was either a stillborn or died from asphyxiation.

In 1921, Daniel French and his daughter Ada Thompson French occupied the house.

Unidentified Adult Male – John Doe

February 11, 1956

Unionville, Connecticut

The individual is a hitchhiker who was killed in a two-car crash.

The individual is described as a 45-year-old white male, weighing 135 pounds, thin build, brown hair, with a scar on his right calf.

The individual wore a white and black checker sports shirt, suede jacket, blue jersey sweater, dark blue pleated pants, and brown shoes.

Oscar Huff, the driver of one of the cars involved in the crash, said he picked the hitchhiker up in Burlington, Connecticut, before the crash.

Unidentified Adult Male – John Doe

1957

North Haven, Connecticut

The skeleton of a white male in his 70's was found in a brook located by a railroad worker's campsite in North Haven, Connecticut, by three rabbit hunters from New Haven, Connecticut.

The individual is described as a white male, 5-10" inches tall, weighing 173 pounds, and wearing rough work clothes and railroad shoes.

Unidentified Adult Male – John Doe

1965

Connecticut River

The badly decomposed body of a man between the ages of 40 - 65 was found in the Connecticut River not far from Colts Street.

According to the Hartford Courant, the body is believed to have been in the water for about a month.

The man was missing his three upper teeth, and wore a white shirt with blue checks, black pants, and crepe-sole shoes with slits near the small toe on each side.

Unidentified Adult Male – John Doe

September 03, 1966

Connecticut River

A skeleton was found 25 feet from the west bank of the Connecticut River, opposite Route I-91.

The individual wore a T-shirt, dark suit jacket, pants, and black low-cut ripple-sole shoes.

No other information is available.

Unidentified Adult Males – John Doe

April 14, 1969

Kent, Connecticut - Homicides

A couple looking for a campsite discovered two bound and burnt bodies on an isolated dirt road near the Housatonic River in Kent, Connecticut.

It is speculated the bodies had been there for approximately three months and could be part of a gangland killing,

Both individuals had their feet bound together with heavy rope; one had his arms tied to his sides and was wearing two winter gloves.

The other individual wore low-cut shoes, a short blue jacket with a zipper, a chain with a gold cross, and one winter glove.

Male – John Doe

Glastonbury, Connecticut Unidentified Adult

April 23, 1969

The individual is a 55-65-year-old white male, 5-09" inches tall, weighing 170 pounds.

The body was found in the Connecticut River and had been in the water for approximately six months.

The individual wore black leather shoes, heavy socks, and a red-striped shirt.

The individual's right arm had a tattoo of three naked females. His left arm had a symbol of a bird wing and the word "Ward" on it.

The individual had a hernia operation near the left side of his groin; no cause of death has been determined.

Unidentified Adult Male – John Doe

August 10, 1986

Connecticut River-Charter Oak Bridge

The individual is described as a white male 50-60 years old, 5-04"
tall, wearing a dungaree jacket, long-sleeve shirt, blue cardigan
sweater, and a gray and brown pair of pants held up by a blue
suspender

The body had been in the water for six to eight months.

Criminal Profile of an Abductor

An essential part of a police investigation into cold case disappearances is to create a suspect profile and abduction patterns.

This is done by reviewing past and current disappearances within a specific geographical area while attempting to discern motives, victims' similarities, and the suspect Modus of Operandi.

Stranger abductions are rare. It is essential to interview as many of the victims' friends and relatives as possible to understand better the people and acquaintances the victim knew or might have recently met.

There appear to be different psychological aspects between the child and adult abductors. However, some of the similarities include control, dominance, and sexual motivation are similar.

The offender often has been a victim of prior physical or sexual violence. The offender has a history of displaying inappropriate sexual behavior against women, being sexually molested as a child; they begin displaying aggressive physical behavior and associated criminal history.

The offender is often a social outcast or socially isolated; the offender is often a substance abuser; suffers from mental health or behavioral issues; and acts selfish and narcissistically by being in control of the victim (Swartz, 2011).

There are two types of stranger offenders: the first act deliberately by selecting specific victims, and the second act opportunistically by selecting random victims (Swartz, 2011).

The stranger offender often fits into two different profiles. The first is the "Power Reassurance Offender," this individual is most often single, is an underachiever, socially odd, displays poor decision-making skills, exhibits low skills, and has a history of sexual fetishes (Swartz, 2011) (Masino and Sheppard, 2006).

The offender chooses his victim based on his need to assert power and control; the abductor sometimes feels attached to the victim and believes the act is occurring with the victim's consent.

The second type of stranger offender is the "Anger Sadistic Offender;" this offender typically has a higher education level and is considered intelligent.

They are accepted socially and are often married or in stable long-term relationships (Swartz, 2011), (Masino and Sheppard, 2006).

The offender will devote a lot of time and resources strategically planning the abduction. The offender chooses his victim to fulfill a complex system of fantasies.

The offender will be deceptive and use trickery to control the victim.

The offender will be emotionless about the abduction or any of the crimes he has committed during the kidnapping (Swartz, 2011) (Masino and Sheppard, 2006).

The "Power Reassurance" abductor's fear of being caught is the motivation factor for committing a homicide. The offender believes the murder will silence the witness, and by hiding the body, he will escape prosecution and distance himself from the crime.

The "Anger Sadistic" offender acts emotionless and will murder and hide the body, not because of fear of being caught, but to reassure his ability to fit back into society while plotting future crimes.

The "Anger Sadistic" offender will often develop a profile of the victim's characteristics before making an abduction; the victim's face is based on the offender's overall goal (Dafinoiu, 2011).

While conducting interviews during the research for this book, the author noticed one common denominator concerning people of interest in each of the cases.

The people of interest were either physically or sexually abused as a child. As adolescents, they began to develop abusive patterns against family members and other non-related people.

Early age trauma would explain the violent acts perpetrated against the victim, a need for personal revenge for the trauma they experienced as a child.

In a more significant percentage of child abductions, the offender suffers from substantial emotional or physiological defects; in many cases, these mental defects include deviant sexual behavior, which plays a crucial role in who the offender selected as a victim.

In most child abduction cases, the offender is sexually fixated on young children seeking sexual gratification. The offender is callous about the child's welfare and is willing to use violence (Duenwald, 2002), (Prentky, 1991).

Violence is a defining factor when determining the psychological profile of a child abductor. We often think of every child abductor as a pedophile, but this is not the case.

The word pedophile is a technical term meaning "Lover of children," the pedophile selects children not only for sexual gratification but for companionship, as well; a true pedophile would be mortified at the thought of harming a child (Duenwald, 2002) (Prentky, 1991).

The sexual predator is motivated by mere sexual gratification and rationalizes using force for submission.

The offender rationalizes the use of force and convinces themself the victim wants to have sex, and the victim is why the offender is required to use force (Duenwald, 2002), (Prentky, 1991), the child is often murdered to hide the crime.

Psychologists warn against focusing only on the small number of children abducted by strangers because it draws the attention away from the larger problem of the more significant number of children being sexually abused by family members and acquaintances (Finkelhor, 2000).

Response to Criminal Abductions

The success in finding an abducted child is based on time, and as any seasoned investigator will tell you, "Time either works for you or against you."

Today's predator stalks children are much more transient and technologically advanced than in the past.

The public views the victims as a mere posters on a telephone pole. The missing person is much more to the people who know and love them (Freeh, 2016).

The number of stranger abductions is much lower than that of children abducted by family members; however, 74% of the children abducted by strangers are murdered after being abducted. Child abduction is a crime that impacts the whole community.

When a parent discovers a child is missing, they should immediately contact the authorities.

Before the police arrive, the parent or guardian should have the information listed.

- Child's full name
- Child's height and weight
- Photograph of the child (Most recent)
- Child's age and date of birth
- Identifying features (Scares, marks, tattoos, or glasses)
- The clothes the child was last seen wearing
- Health issues
- Jewelry
- Names and contact numbers of the child's relatives and friends
- Place where the child often hangs out
- Any other relevant information, history of running away, new acquaintances, or strangers

While on the scene, the law enforcement personnel should immediately place a radio broadcast to other patrol units with the child/adult's physical description and clothing. Additional radio broadcasts with any additional information should be continuously made.

The sooner the information is put out over the air. The mobile patrol unit can begin canvassing where the child was last seen. The search pattern should start where the child was last seen and extend outwards.

This includes areas where the child often frequents,

Additional information about possible suspects/acquaintances allows police officers to focus on specific locations or dwellings where possible suspects or suspect vehicles may be found within the search perimeter.

Family and friends will often know new acquaintances or friends who the victim has recently met.

All disappearance cases should be considered criminal until proven otherwise. To coin a phrase, "If it doesn't look right, it probably isn't right."

An essential aspect of the investigation is time. It either works for you or against you, as I have previously stated in this publication and several other books. If you have any information concerning a missing person or a murder victim, you must inform law enforcement or have someone notify the authorities. You have become a conspirator in the crime.

Family members of missing or murdered people have the right to know.

References

Balalis, Nicholas I.
2016
Forensic Autopsy of Blunt
Force Trauma, Medscape.

Bouchard, Michael C.
2016
Forever Searching – Missing in
the Great Smoky Mountains,
Kindle Direct Publishing.

Dafinoiu, David V.
2011
The Psychology of Kidnapping
and Abduction, *Security News
Center.*

Duenward, Mary
2002
Who Would Abduct a Child?
Previous Cases Offer Clues,
Science.

Finkelhor, David
2000
Children Abduction Patterns,
Profiles and Prevention.

Greif, Geoffrey Ph. D
2012
The Impact of Child Abduction
on Families – Ambiguous Loss
and Child Abduction, Baltimore
Sun.

Hamilton, Jesse
2002
1975 Homicide Revisited, The
Hartford Courant.

Holmes, Lucy
2008
Living in Limbo: The Experiences
of, and Impacts on, the Families
of Missing People.

McKenna, R., Brown, K. M, Keppel, R. D, Weis, J, and Skeen, M.
2006
Case Management for Missing
Children Homicide Investigation.

References

Miller, J., Kurlycheck, M., Hansen, J. and Wilson, K.
2008   Examining Child Abduction by Offender Type Patterns.

Prentky, R.A.   Molesters Who Abduct, Research
1991   Department, Massachusetts.

Ressler, R. K.   Sexual Homicide: Patterns and
1998   Motives.

Sedlak, A., Finkelhor, D., Hammer, H., and Schultz, D.
2002   National Estimates of Missing Children: an Overview.

Shugarts, Jonathan   A Look Inside Connecticut's
2015   Cold Case Unit.

Swartz, Daniel   Profiling Abductors Q&A with
2011   Brad Garrett, CBC News.

Wayland, Sarah

2007   Holding on to Hope: A Review of Literature Exploring Missing Hope and Ambiguous Loss, University of Technology Sydney.

Reoccurring References

Connecticut 2017	National Center for Missing and Exploited Children.
NamUs 2017	National Missing and Unidentified Person System.
Reddit 2017	Unsolved Mysteries – Missing in Connecticut Online Series.
The Charley Project 2017	The Charley Project.
The Doe Network 2017	The Doe Network, 420 Airport Road Livingston, Tennessee.
Wikipedia 2017	Free Online Encyclopedia by the Wikimedia Foundation.

Personal Interviews

Baldwin, Bernadette
2018

Susan LaRosa Sister

Engelbrecht, Mary
2017

Janice Pockett's Sister

Givens, Robert
2018

Detective – Connecticut State
Police

Gunthier, Anne
2018

Susan Larosa's Older Sister

Shanks, Terr
2018

Susan LaRosa's Younger Sister

Kelly, Gerald
2018

Lisa Joy White's Stepfather

Prentiss, Barry E.
2018

Ex- Brother-in-Law (Susan
Gunthier LaRosa)

LaRosa, Debbie
2018

Rudy, Nathan, and Robert
LaRosa's Younger Sister

LaRosa, Rudy
2017

Nunzio "*Nathan*" LaRosa Jr., and
Robert LaRosa Sr.'s Brother

LaRosa-Beebe, Stacy
2017

Susan LaRosa and Robert LaRosa
Sr. Daughter

Richburg, Tina
2017

Irene LaRosa's Niece

Prentiss, Barry E. Sr.
2018

Robert LaRosa ex Brother-in-
Law

Social and Media Sources

de Sturler, Alice
2018

Defrostingcoldcases.com

Sutten, Terry
2018

Cold Cases (Connecticut)
Investigative Journalist

Author's Page

Michael C. Bouchard

True Crime:

The Disappearance of Dennis Lloyd Martin – Lost in the Smoky Mountains
The Disappearance of Joan Carolyn Risch: Case #6162
The Connecticut Cult – The Broken Cross
Cop Stories – Unconscious Decisions
Missing in Connecticut – Missing and Unidentified Persons

Science Fiction:

Creatures of Folklore – Fact or Fiction

Mystery:

The Covered Bridge – The Map of the Future
The Police Car Conspiracy

Archaeology:

The Paleo Project – A Review and Interpretation of Paleo -Indian Distribution
Patterns in Connecticut
The Archaeology and Ecology of the Laurel Beach Encampment
The Baldwin Station Site and Its Environs
The Joshua Bouchard Site – An Isolated Frontenac Workshop in Shelton,
Connecticut

Anchor Radio: Host of The Night Stalker series.
Amazon: Author Central
Contact: Forevernightct1@comcast.net
LinkedIn: Michael C. Bouchard

Printed in Great Britain
by Amazon

27872500R00138